Day by Day in Ephesians

Don E. Atkinson

Day by day
in the Word

ISBN: 978-1-941733-39-4

All Scripture quotations, unless otherwise indicated, are taken from the *New American Standard Bible ®*, 1960, 1962, 1963, 1968, 1971, 1972, 1973, 1975, 1977, 1995 by The Lockman Foundation. Used by permission. www.Lockman.org.

Scripture quotations marked KJV are taken from the King James Version.

Cover created by: BelieversBookServices

Cover revised by: Andrew Cullen

Cover aerial photograph from the Austrian Archaeological Institute, released into the public domain.

Cover photography shows ruins of the Great Theater of ancient Ephesus. The Arcadian Way led from the ancient harbor of Ephesus west to this open air Greek-Roman amphitheater. A short segment of the Arcadian Way in front of the Great Theater can be seen on the bottom portion of the back cover.

Published by EA Books Publishing a division of

Living Parables of Central Florida, Inc. a 501c3

EABooksPublishing.com

To Ira Donald Atkinson

My beloved father
A WWII veteran
A bran packer at Gooch's Mill
But most of all a Christian dad given by God!

CONTENTS

Contents

Contents

Contents

Contents

ACKNOWLEDGMENTS

I am deeply grateful to Jon Atkinson, my identical twin, who continually encouraged me as I planned and wrote this daily devotional. His assistance and support with editing and related tasks were invaluable as I struggled at times through the numerous steps of the editing process.

In addition, I am thankful to Larry Ganshorn who edited parts of the manuscript and to Julie Ieron, of Believers Book Services, who conducted the first full edit of my manuscript. Further, I wish to thank Andrew Mackay, of Believers Book Services, for helping me generate typesetting notes, helping me select typefaces and leading, and for designing my cover.

I have greatly appreciated all the positive, professional and encouraging assistance provided to me by staff members of EA Books Publishing. Specifically, I wish to thank Jessie Collins for her professional formatting of my devotional, and Bob Ousnamer for his encouragement and professional work designing my web page.

In addition, I express my gratitude to Andrew Cullen who patiently, creatively, and artistically worked with me in the development of the Day by Day in the Word ministry logo and later revised both the front and back covers.

I am deeply indebted to my wife, Diane, who listened to me as I initially expressed my sense of being led to write the devotional. Subsequently, she has listened to me and expressed her concern and support as I wrote, edited, and rewrote the devotional. Also, her prayers for me and this literary endeavor have been much appreciated.

PREFACE

Welcome to *Day by Day in Ephesians*. This daily devotional is a product of Day by Day in the Word, a nonprofit, nondenominational Christian ministry. You are to be commended for selecting a daily devotional that deals exclusively with just one book of the New Testament.

Providing all the daily devotionals from the same biblical book has merit for Christians for at least three reasons. First, *context* (literary, historical, political) is a vital element in correctly interpreting and applying Scripture in the twenty-first century that was written in the first century AD. Consequently, I have included two introductions—one to the NT and one to the epistle of Ephesians. In addition, because all the devotionals are based on verses in Ephesians, they revolve around verses having the same context. Second, each book of the Bible has a geographical context as well as a cultural context. Therefore, you will find a map of Asia Minor on page 15. Third, continuity or organization of a devotional is important. This devotional follows, verse-by-verse, the content of Ephesians—which is God's flow of thought.

As you read and reflect on the devotionals, you will be exposed to *theological themes* such as:

- the nature of salvation

- unity of all believers

- how the gospel relates to the mystery of God

- the universal church or the body of Christ

It is the author's desire that you will draw closer to God as you better understand the spiritual blessings God included in your salvation. Some of God's spiritual blessings include:

- being chosen in Christ before foundation of the world   1:4
- though dead, you were made alive with Christ   2:5
- you were predestined to adoption   1:5
- you received redemption through Christ's blood   1:7
- you were sealed in Christ with the Holy Spirit   1:13
- you are Christ's workmanship created for good works   2:10
- you were chosen to be holy   1:4

Further, I trust this devotional will:

- help you see God and His only begotten Son, Jesus, more clearly so you will be transformed by His Word and the Holy Spirit;
- equip you to discover truths concerning what the Godhead planned for your salvation;
- encourage you to assimilate these truths into your heart and *apply* them in practical ways in your daily life.

May you "grow in the grace and knowledge of our Lord and Savior Jesus Christ" (2 Peter 3:18) as you read, reflect on, and apply the truths God presents in His epistle to the Ephesians.

—Don E. Atkinson

SCRIPTURE ABBREVIATIONS

Genesis	Gen.	Isaiah	Is.
1 Corinthians	1 Cor.	Colossians	Col.
Exodus	Ex.	Jeremiah	Jer.
2 Corinthians	2 Cor.	1 Thessalonians	1Thess.
Leviticus	Lev.	Isaiah	Is.
Galatians	Gal.	Hebrews	Heb.
Psalms	Ps.	Matthew	Matt.
Ephesians	Eph.	1 Timothy	1 Tim.
Proverbs	Prov.	Romans	Rom.
Philippians	Phil.	2 Timothy	2 Tim.
Revelation	Rev.		

THE ROMAN PROVINCE OF ASIA

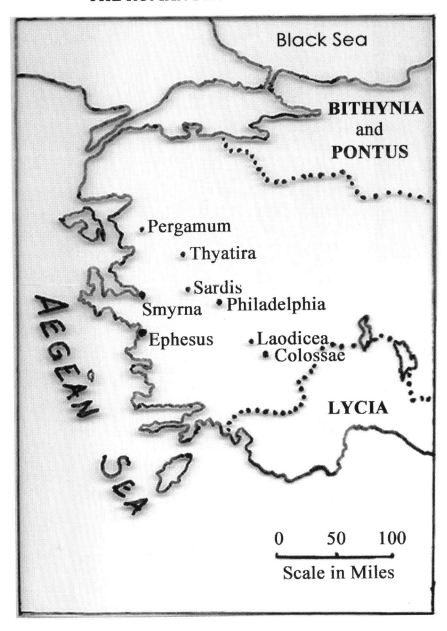

Included are the two small provinces of Bithynia and Pontus and Lycia.

HOW TO USE THE DAILY DEVOTIONAL

At the top of each devotional is a title. Below the title is the Scripture for the day taken from the *New American Standard Bible* (NASB). After the Scripture quotation, I have prepared a brief, biblically based discussion of that Scripture. Each day closes with a Thought for the Day.

It is my desire that you receive the maximum spiritual encouragement and blessing from each one of these devotionals. Therefore, I encourage you to set aside time at least five days a week for your devotional time. To begin each quiet time, I recommend you start with prayer, asking God to reveal truth or truths to you, as He wills. I suggest you start by reading the Scripture for the day slowly and reflecting on it. After slowly reading the Scripture discussion, prayerfully reflect on the biblical truths presented. Please allow God to give you additional thoughts from the discussion of Scripture, as He wills.

As you read the Thought for the Day, consider and honestly analyze your relationship with Jesus as well as your spiritual maturity. Ask God to help you apply any new insights to *your* life. Then end your quiet time with additional prayer and thanksgiving to God for His many blessings.

These are merely some general recommendations. You are encouraged to alter them as necessary to maximize the spiritual benefits and encouragement you receive from your quiet times.

INTRODUCTION TO THE
NEW TESTAMENT AND EPHESIANS

NEW TESTAMENT

In the OT, God promised Israel that someday He would make a new covenant (testament) with His people (Jer. 31:31–34). Jesus came to earth and established that new testament through His life, death, and resurrection. As a result, the sacred writings that relate to Him and His church, make up the NT.

The New Testament consists of twenty-seven books and divides into four sections:

- The Gospels

- The Acts of the Apostles

- The Epistles (letters)

- Revelation

EPISTLE TO THE EPHESIANS

Author

This epistle was written by Paul the apostle (1:1; 3:1). This had been the accepted view throughout church history until the nineteenth and twentieth centuries. In more recent years, scholars have debated its authorship. Today half of the Bible scholars deny Pauline authorship.

When Written

Paul wrote Ephesians in approximately AD 60–62 near the end of his life, while in prison in Rome.

Introduction

Purpose

It is not easy to find any problem or occasion that called for this epistle. It probably was written for instructing and edifying Christians over a wide geographical area (western Asia Minor). This assumption is supported by the fact that Paul dealt with the broad subject of God's majestic saving purposes in the first half of his epistle. In the second half, he gave exhortations regarding a variety of subjects. He intended to inform, strengthen, and encourage Gentile Christian readers by assuring them of their place within the saving purpose of God. Then he urged them to bring their lives into conformity with this divine plan. Paul did this to ground and challenge his readers in their faith.

Audience

Ephesians was probably intended as a circular letter to be passed from church to church in western Asia Minor. Paul wrote this letter to mainly Gentile Christians for whom he had apostolic responsibilities.

Historical Setting

Of all the Pauline epistles, Ephesians is the most general and the least situational. It does not have the urgency of Paul's other letters. The apostle assumed his readers knew him (1:1; 3:1; 6:21, 22) as well as his sufferings and imprisonment (3:13; 4:1).

Ancient Ephesus was four miles inland from the Aegean Sea on the west coast of modern-day Turkey. It was the capital of the Roman province of Asia, a commercial and political center for the area. Also, it is one of the seven churches Jesus addressed in Revelation 1–2.

Many pagan religions were practiced in Ephesus. The temple of Artemis (Diana), the largest building known in antiquity, was located there. This temple was considered one of the seven wonders of the ancient world.

Introduction

Outline

Key Theological Themes

1. The nature of salvation: In His eternal purpose, God planned, executed, sustained, and directed the salvation of mankind (chapter 1).
2. Jew and Gentile are now one in Christ—unity of believers (chapter 2; 4:4).
3. The gospel and how it relates to the mystery of God (1:9; chapter 3; 5:32).
4. Teachings about Christian living (chapters 4–6).
5. Doctrine of the universal church and the church as Christ's body (1:22–23) and the body (4:4).

Introduction

Types of Writing within Ephesians

1.	Eulogy	1:3–14
2.	Prayers of Thanksgiving	1:15–23; 3:14–19
3.	Didactic (instructional) materials	2:1–22; 3:1–13; 4:3–16
4.	Doxology	3:20–21
5.	Reprimand	4:17–19
6.	Encouragement	1:15; 5:1–2
7.	Commands	4:1–3; 17–32; 5:1–11;15–33; 6:1–19

GRACE AND PEACE TO YOU FROM GOD

Paul, an apostle of Christ Jesus by the will of God, to the saints who are at Ephesus and who are faithful in Christ Jesus: 2 Grace to you and peace from God our Father and the Lord Jesus Christ.—**Eph. 1:1–2**

The title apostle designated somebody chosen, called, and sent to teach with authority. Paul's apostleship was derived from the will of God and from the commission of Jesus. Therefore, Paul's authority as a teacher was the authority of Jesus Christ.

The term saints refers to all God's true children. Paul called his readers saints because they had been set apart by God and belonged to Jesus.

Paul used the phrase *faithful in Christ Jesus* to characterize his readers, united by their common faith in God through Jesus Christ. "In Christ Jesus" indicates his readers are personally and individually united to Christ. Therefore, they relate individually to the Head (Jesus) of the body and to its other members.

In verse 2, Paul introduced two profound theological concepts—grace and peace. Grace can be defined as God's unmerited (undeserved) favor in providing salvation for sinners through Christ's sacrificial death. Also, grace can be described as God's enabling power. Paul wanted the Ephesians to appropriate God's grace, or undeserved favor into their lives.

Peace has the idea of sinners' peace with God (2:14) and believers' peace with one another (2:15; 4:3). Grace is the cause of God's gracious work and peace is its effect.

Thought for the Day: If you are a saint (a child of God), are you experiencing daily the grace (enabling power) and peace of God? If not, accept and appropriate God's grace today.

EULOGY, PART I—PRAISE TO THE FATHER

Blessed be the God and Father of our Lord Jesus Christ, who has blessed us with every spiritual blessing in the heavenly places in Christ—Eph. 1:3

After the brief introduction, Paul gave an extended eulogy (vv. 3–14). This eulogy is outlined around the three persons of the Trinity with the phrase, "to the praise of his glory" ending each section or strophe (vv. 6, 12 and 14). In verses 3–6, Paul praised the Father who blessed us (v. 3), chose us (v. 4), and predestined us to adoption as sons (v. 5).

God the **Father** is the source of every blessing we enjoy. The Father's initiative in choosing believers is clearly seen in verses 3–6. Verse 3 is a summary of the eulogy. Paul informed his readers that Jehovah is both the God and Father of our Lord Jesus Christ. This truth is important because it indicates that Jesus is the Son of God.

Blessed us with every spiritual blessing

In the Greek language, the verb *blessed* is in the past tense. This gives the idea of the past activity of God. These blessings of the new covenant are spiritual, not physical. These spiritual blessings:

- have their source in the Spirit of God

- are applicable at the present time to believers

- are supernatural

Examples of such spiritual blessing are our personal knowledge of God and the forgiveness of our sins. Therefore, God has blessed the believer with every spiritual blessing needed for his or her spiritual well-being.

In the heavenly places

With this prepositional phrase, no geographical location is implied. It refers to the unseen world of spiritual reality. *Heavenly places* gives the sphere:

- where the principalities and powers continue to operate   3:10; 6:12
- where Christ reigns at the right hand of God   1:20

- of the present position of believers in relationship to Christ   2:6
- where God blesses believers with every spiritual blessing   1:3

In Christ indicates the *place* where believers are located and the place in whom salvation is found.

Thought for the Day: As a believer, are you praising God daily because you have been blessed with "every spiritual blessing" needed for your spiritual well-being?

Notes:

_____

_____

_____

_____

_____

_____

EULOGY, PART II—GOD CHOSE YOU TO BE HOLY

Just as He chose us in Him before the foundation of the world, that we would be holy and blameless before Him.—**Eph. 1:4**

The concepts *chose* (v. 4) and *predestined* (v. 5) make up what is often called the doctrine of *election*. In verse 4, we learn that God determined to make us (who did not yet exist) His children through the redeeming work of Christ. The verb *chose* in the Greek is in the past tense. Paul told his readers how far in the past God did His choosing: "before the foundation of the world."

In Him indicates that God chose us in connection with Christ. In other words, God chose believers through Christ's work of redemption. God chose the believer for His glory and His choosing had to be done in connection with the redemption that was accomplished by Christ's death and His bodily resurrection.

Here **holy** signifies being separated from sin and therefore consecrated to God. Consequently, holiness is the *purpose* of the believer's election.

The Greek word blameless means "without blemish." God chose believers that they might be *holy* and *without blame*. Here, Paul probably was referring to the process of "progressive sanctification" that can begin as soon as one becomes a believer. In this process, believers become more like Christ as they read, study, and memorize the Word, pray, confess their sin, and fellowship with other believers.

In summary, the **goal** for which God chose His people in Christ is that they should be holy and blameless before Him. This fulfills God's intention for humankind—to create for Himself a people conformed to the likeness of His Son (Rom. 8:29–30).

Thought for the Day: As a believer, are you advancing toward the purpose of your election—personal holiness (Hebrews 12:14)

EULOGY, PART III—PREDESTINED TO ADOPTION

In love **5** He predestined us to adoption as sons through
Jesus Christ to Himself, according to the kind intention
of His will—**Eph. 1:5**

The Greek word for predestined means "to mark out beforehand."

Under Roman law, the procedure of adoption had two steps. First, the son had to be released from the control of his natural father. The father sold him three times to the adopter. The adopter would release him two times. With the third sale, the adoptee was freed from his natural father. Second, because the natural father no longer had authority over the son, the adopter became the new father with absolute control over him. The new father retained this control until the adoptee died or the adopter freed him. The son was responsible only to his new father. Adoption in the time of Paul allowed the adoptee to take the position of a natural son to continue the family line.

In light of **physical** or natural adoption, we will look at **spiritual** adoption. First, believers, now have no responsibility to their old father, the *devil*. Second, they are now God's sons and daughters; He controls their lives and property. Their allegiance to their new Father, God, supersedes all prior allegiances. Third, the Father has a right to discipline His sons (Heb. 12:5–11). Fourth, the one adopted acquires a new status, privilege, property, and responsibilities. What a contrast between these two spiritual fathers!

According to the good pleasure of His will gives the reason for God's action on our behalf.

In summary, God "predestined us to adoption" as sons and daughters in His family through His Son, Jesus (v. 5).

Thought for the Day: As a believer, are you thankful that God adopted you into His family?

EULOGY, PART IV—PRAISE
FOR THE GLORY OF GOD'S GRACE

To the praise of the glory of His grace, which He freely bestowed on us in the Beloved.—**Eph. 1:6**

The panorama of blessings Paul listed in verse 3 continues in verse 6. This is the first occurrence of the refrain, "to the praise of His glory." Here, Paul added the prepositional phrase, "of His grace." Verse 6 marks the end of the first stanza in Paul's eulogy of praise that revolves around God the Father.

All the actions of the Father (vv. 3–5) have as their goal the *praise of God*. Praise refers to the praise that believers offer God.

Glory is the reflection of the essence of one's being. God's essential being is the sum of all His attributes or qualities.

Grace refers to God's unmerited favor in providing salvation for sinners through Christ's sacrificial death. God's eternal election of grace is the election of Jesus. Jesus is the Elect One from eternity past.

With the clause "that He freely bestowed on us," Paul was referring to an objective bestowal of grace on the believers.

Beloved is a title for Jesus that is used only here in the NT. This title marks Jesus as the supreme object of the Father's love. Also, this title continues the idea that all God's blessings come to Christians "in Christ." Further, this title for Jesus serves as a transition from the blessings of the Father (vv. 3–6) to the blessings of the Son (vv. 7–12), which is the subject of the second stanza of Paul's eulogy of praise.

Thought for the Day: As a believer, are you praising God daily for His grace because you are in Christ or "in the Beloved"?

10

GOD'S REDEMPTION IS IN CHRIST

In Him we have redemption through His blood, the forgiveness of
our trespasses, according to the riches of His grace—**Eph. 1:7**

The second stanza of Paul's eulogy of praise (vv. 7–12) deals
with redemption, forgiveness, and inheritance in Christ.

In verse 7 we learn God provides **redemption** in Christ. The
concept of redemption has roots in slavery during OT times.
Redemption describes the release of slaves (Ex. 21:8; Lev. 25:48).
In NT times, a slave still could be bought out of slavery with a
ransom or payment price. *Redemption* requires the payment of a
ransom price to purchase the slave's release. **Have** is in the
present tense, meaning redemption is an ongoing state;
redemption and forgiveness are present possessions. Here, the
emphasis is on "setting free" rather than "payment" (ransom).

This phrase **through His blood** states the *cost* of the ransom.
Christ's violent death on the cross as a sacrifice is the only means
by which our deliverance could be achieved. Redemption and
ransom show the costliness of human salvation.

Forgiveness further defines redemption. "Forgiveness of sins"
is the immediate result of redemption—the release from sin's
bondage. Forgiveness deals with the objective offense standing
between a person and God. To forgive someone is to release him
from obligation; it includes the idea of freedom. God's forgiveness
is essential to our restored relationship with the Father.

The divine "riches of His grace" are the ultimate *cause* of our
redemption. The wealth of God's grace was necessary to redeem
and forgive the sinner.

Thought for the Day: Thank God today that He gave His
Son so you could be redeemed—not with perishable
things, "but with the precious blood of Christ" (1 Peter 1:18–
19).

PRAISE FOR THE MYSTERY OF HIS WILL

Which He lavished on us. In all wisdom and insight **9** He made known
to us the mystery of His will, according to His kind intention which
He purposed in Him **10** with a view to an administration suitable to
the fullness of the times, that is, the summing up of all things in
Christ, things in the heavens and things on the earth.—**Eph. 1:8–10**

The generous bestowal ("lavished on us") of God's grace
accompanies other blessings, including God making known to
each Christian **the mystery of His will**. Each Christian can
experience the mystery of His will.

Mystery refers to something in ages past that was hidden in God
(3:9) and unable to be understood by human study. However, now it
has been revealed by the Holy Spirit to His holy apostles and
prophets (3:4, 5), who then made it known to others. The recipients
of this disclosure are individual members of the Church. The mystery
also refers to the end times fulfillment of God's plan of salvation in
Christ.

according to His kind intention which He purposed in Him

God's revelation of His mysterious plan of salvation was
compatible with His sovereign and eternal purpose. Before the
foundation of the world (1:4), God determined His eternal purpose
for humanity would be accomplished in Christ.

Administration refers to how God is working out His purpose
through human history—past, present and future. While the content
of the mystery has been revealed (v. 9), the *outworking* of God's
saving purposes (summing up of all things in Christ) is far from
completed.

The phrase **suitable to the fullness of times** relates to a time
when God will unite under one head (Christ) all of creation. This will
probably occur during Christ's *messianic rule*.

The phrase things in the heavens and things on earth shows that
God's purposes reach beyond human beings to include the rest of a
fractured creation—"things in the heavens and things on the earth."
Currently, the whole creation is groaning. In contrast, God will

eventually provide the day of release from the curse of sin (Rom. 8:23).

Thought for the Day: Are you praising God for His revealed "mystery," His plan of salvation in Christ?

Notes:

_____

_____

_____

_____

_____

_____

PRAISE FOR THE BELIEVER'S INHERITANCE

In Him **11** also we have obtained an inheritance, having been predestined according to His purpose who works all things after the counsel of His will, **12** to the end that we who were the first to hope in Christ would be to the praise of His glory.—**Eph. 1:11–12**

Here Paul introduced the theological concept of *inheritance*. Some believe by the clause **obtained an inheritance** Paul was referring to what believers receive from God—an inheritance in the kingdom of God (5:5). Others believe the Christian is God's possession, being God's inheritance. Christians become God's heritage because their destiny as His inheritance was predestined by Him.

The phrase "who works all things" after counsel of His will refers to the working out of God's will in the lives of believers. *All things* refers to all aspects of God's providence and should not be restricted only to God's plan of salvation.

By the phrase, **after the counsel of His will**, Paul communicated the deliberation on God's part. Therefore, God's plans and decisions were not based on mere whims. Verse 11 can be paraphrased: "Believers are God's heritage because He *predestined* them and powerfully works out His purpose for believers according to His providence and His deliberative will."

Those of Jewish origin, were the *first* to accept the Lord Jesus Christ. Therefore, **we** in verses 11 and 12 probably referred to Paul, his fellow Jewish believers, and to Jesus' original disciples.

Because of this "hope in Christ," early Jewish Christians praised God and His glory. Now all Christians are to praise God and His glory.

Thought for the Day: Today reflect on the glorious truth that as a Christian, you are God's possession and have "an inheritance" in the kingdom of God.

14

GOD'S SEAL WITH THE SPIRIT

In Him, you also, after listening to the message of truth, the gospel
of your salvation—having also believed, you were sealed in Him with
the Holy Spirit of promise.—**Eph. 1:13**

Having stated the Father's plan (1:3–6) and the Son's provision for that plan (1:7–12), Paul then discussed the Holy Spirit's ministry. This ministry is to make salvation a reality in all those who believe—Jews and Gentiles.

You also refers to Gentile believers at Ephesus. Further, the you of verse 13 extends to Christians of all ages, races and both genders. Paul used *truth* for the content of Christianity as the absolute truth.

By "the gospel of your salvation," Paul was referring to the message itself, sometimes called the *good news*. "Salvation" indicates rescue or deliverance.

Not only hearing but *believing* the message of truth is necessary for salvation.

you were sealed with the Holy Spirit of promise

"Sealed" is in the past tense. This shows that the Gentile believers were sealed with the Holy Spirit in the past when they believed the gospel. Further, the Holy Spirit is the instrument or the means of the seal. The sealing ministry of the Spirit is to identify believers as God's own and give them the security that they belong to Him. This truth regarding sealing applied to the believers (Jewish and Gentile) in Bible times, and applies to all believers in Christ **today**.

In summary, first the Ephesians heard the gospel, then they believed the gospel and subsequently, they were "sealed" in Christ with the Holy Spirit.

Thought for the Day: Today stop and reflect on the sealing ministry of the Holy Spirit and thank God because you are owned by Him.

SEALED UNTIL REDEMPTION

Who is given as a pledge of our inheritance, with a view to the redemption of God's own possession, to the praise of His glory.—**Eph. 1:14**

Yesterday we learned that when the Ephesians heard the gospel and believed they were sealed in Christ with the Holy Spirit. Today we will learn more about the functions of the Holy Spirit, the third person of the Trinity.

In verse 14, Paul tells us the Holy Spirit was given to believers as an earnest or **pledge**. The word *pledge* is used of earnest money—a down payment forfeited if the purchase is not completed. In this case, the Holy Spirit is the first installment on the believer's inheritance, with God's guarantee that the rest will follow at Jesus' second coming.

pledge of our inheritance

Here and in 5:5, *inheritance* refers to the eternal inheritance of heaven. In previous verses, we learned the believer's inheritance or gain of heaven is made possible by:

• the Father's election	vv. 4–5
• the Son's redemption	v. 7
• the Spirit's sealing	v. 13

This inheritance qualifies believers to live eternally in heaven in the presence of God. What an eternal blessing!

with a view to the redemption of God's possession

Here, Paul referred to believers as "God's own possession" because He has:

• chosen them in Christ	v. 4
• redeemed them in Christ	v. 7
• adopted them as sons through Jesus	v. 5

16

Paul used redemption in verses 7 and 14 to stress two aspects of redemption. In verse 7, Paul gave the *effect* of redemption as "the forgiveness of our sins." In verse 14, Paul stressed the idea of God *setting free* His possession.

to the praise of His glory

This refrain, similar to those he has used twice earlier, marks the end of the third and last stanza of Paul's eulogy.

Thought for the Day: Praise God that because of your spiritual inheritance, you will live eternally in heaven in the presence of God.

Notes:

_____

_____

_____

_____

_____

_____

A PRAYER OF THANKSGIVING FOR THE EPHESIANS

For this reason I too, having heard of the faith in the Lord Jesus which exists among you and your love for all the saints, 16 do not cease giving thanks for you—**Eph. 1:15–16a**

The first part (vv. 15–16a) of Paul's prayer for his Ephesian readers (vv. 15–23) consists of *thanksgiving* for the Ephesians.

With the phrase **for this reason**, Paul was probably looking back to the previous paragraph where he discussed spiritual blessings (vv. 3–14, especially vv. 13–14) that God had bestowed upon them—primarily redemption.

In addition, Paul thanked God for his readers because of their "faith in the Lord Jesus" and their "love for all the saints." He had spent nearly three years in Ephesus. However, he had not been in Ephesus for five to six years. Consequently, there were many new believers with whom Paul had no personal acquaintance. Their *faith in the Lord Jesus* probably refers to their initial act of faith, as well as to their continuing faith in Jesus.

The expression **all the saints** signifies Christians generally, Jews and Gentiles. Therefore, the Gentile readers' "love for all the saints" is proof that the ancestral barrier between Jew and Gentile was being broken down in Christ.

God's love seeks the highest good in the one loved. It is only through God's love that Christians, sinners saved by God's grace, are enabled to serve one another. Consequently, Paul assured his readers that he was constantly "giving thanks" for the divine work that had been accomplished in their lives (v. 16a).

Thought for the Day: Do you usually possess the Ephesians' Christ like attitude of love for all believers?

PAUL'S PRAYER FOR THE EPHESIANS

While making mention of you in my prayers; **17** that the God
of our Lord Jesus Christ, the Father of glory, may give to
you a spirit of wisdom and revelation in the knowledge of
Him. **18a** I pray that the eyes of your heart may be
enlightened—**Eph. 1:16b–18a**

In his intercession for the Ephesians (vv. 16b–19), the phrase "the God of our Lord Jesus Christ, the Father of glory" shows the subordination of Jesus, the Son, to the Father.

In the expression **a spirit of wisdom and revelation,** "spirit" probably does not refer to the believer's human spirit but more likely to the Holy Spirit. Here *wisdom* has to do with a knowledge of God's will. "Revelation" refers to a truth that was previously hidden but now has been unveiled such as the mystery of His will (v. 9).

The phrase, **in the knowledge of Him** means to be in a close personal relationship with Him. Further, it begins with a fear of God, is linked with His demands, and is often described as "knowing His will."

In verse 18, Paul continued requesting spiritual understanding for his readers. He used metaphorical language (**eyes of your heart may be enlightened**) to express his desire that the Ephesians may have sufficient spiritual insight to grasp the truth of God's purposes. Then their thought and understanding will be enlightened. "Heart" is used here in the OT sense to describe the seat of the physical, spiritual and mental life.

In this intercessory prayer, Paul asked God to give the Ephesians an additional measure of the Holy Spirit to help them gain insight and revelation. These acquisitions will increase their knowledge of God.

Thought for the Day: How intimately do you know God? Are you studying the Scriptures to know God's will better?

PAUL'S INTERCESSORY PRAYER, PART II

So that you will know what is the hope of His calling, what are
the riches of the glory of His inheritance in the saints, **19**
and what is the surpassing greatness of His power toward us who
believe. These are in accordance with the working of the strength
of His might—**Eph. 1:18b–19**

In these two verses, Paul continued his intercessory prayer by showing concern about the spiritual growth of his readers. He asked God to help them know the:

- hope to which God has called them   v. 18b
- rich inheritance that God possesses in them   v. 18b
- mighty power with which He energizes them   v. 19

Paul wanted God to help the Ephesians understand more fully the **hope** into which God has brought them by His call to salvation. Paul used hope to denote both the *subjective* act of hoping and the *objective* content of the hope that looks back to God's work of redemption. Therefore, the believer's subjective hope is based on objective hope. Some objective spiritual realities Paul could be thinking about include the hope of: one's final salvation, righteousness, resurrection to a glorified body, and eternal life.

In the NT, the concept of "hope" includes three elements: (1) expectation, (2) trust in God, and (3) a patient waiting for God to work out His plan of salvation.

With his words, **the riches of the glory of His inheritance in the saints,** Paul expressed the idea of abundance. God's *inheritance* is located in His saints. The term inheritance indicates believers are valuable to God. He *purchased* them to inherit them. "Hope" produced by His *calling* looks to the *past*—when the believer was called and accepted Jesus as Savior. In contrast, hope produced by looking to "His inheritance in the saints" looks to the future—the hope realized fully at Christ's second coming.

His power ... with the working of the strength of His might

Here Paul referred to the power of God that He directs toward believers *now*. To emphasize the awesomeness of God's power in their lives, Paul used four Greek words for power in verse 19: (1) the greatness of His *power*, (2) in accordance with the *working*, (3) of the *strength*, and (4) of His *might*.

Thought for the Day: Thank God today that He called you and for the infinite hope which is involved in your calling.

Notes:

_____

_____

_____

_____

_____

_____

GOD'S POWER IN RESURRECTING CHRIST

Which He brought about in Christ, when He raised Him
from the dead and seated Him at His right hand
*in the heavenly places—**Eph. 1:20***

In verse 19 Paul discussed God's working in the lives of believers. In contrast, in vv. 20–23, Paul explained how God worked in Christ. In verse 20, Paul picked up on the word "working" that he used in verse 19. In verse 20, the Greek word "working" is translated "**brought about** in Christ." This phrase qualifies "the working of the strength of His might" (v. 19b). It also affirms that God's power, demonstrated in the resurrection and exaltation of Christ, is available to all believers.

In this verse Paul told his readers of two ways God exercised His power toward Christ: (1) **He raised Christ from the dead**; and (2) He "seated Him at His right hand." Power associated with this Greek word (*energeia*) is "active" power.

The clause "He raised Him from the dead" shows the resurrection power of God. This power emanates from Christ as the life-giving force of the new life which Christians experience. Second, when God "seated Him at His right hand," two truths were seen: (1) God's mighty act exalted Christ to a position of unparalleled honor and authority (Matt. 26:64; Heb. 1:3–4); and (2) to be seated at the Father's right hand points to Christ's completion of His God-assigned task.

Christ's resurrection is the vindication of His messiahship and sonship. Christ's exaltation to heaven at the right hand of God is related to the inauguration of His lordship.

Thought for the Day: Reflect on the truth that the power of God uses in the lives of believers is the same might by which He raised Christ from the tomb to share His throne.

CHRIST—HEAD OVER ALL THINGS FOR THE CHURCH

Far above all rule and authority and power and dominion, and every
name that is named, not only in this age but also in the age to come.
22 And He put all things in subjection under His feet, and gave Him
as head over all things to the church, **23** which is His body, the
fullness of Him who fills all in all.—**Eph. 1:21–23**

Christ's position at the right hand of the Father (v. 20) gives
Him the full authority of the Father. Thus, His position is
superior to every hostile "power," in heaven or on earth.

Paul added that Christ has been enthroned above **every name**
that can be given not only in "this age" but also in the "age to come."
Christ's supremacy in *this age* was achieved by His death and
resurrection. The rulers of this age will not exercise any power or
control in the *age to come*.

God has subjected **all things** in creation, animate and inanimate,
under Christ's feet (v. 22). Paul then tied Christ's supremacy with the
truth about God's purpose for Christ in relation to the church. **Head**
denotes the idea of authority. Therefore, Christ has authority over
His *church*.

His body (v. 23) is Paul's figurative language for the *church*. The
term "fullness" is related to God or to Christ. The church is Christ's
fullness and His body. He rules His church or fills it in a special way
with His Spirit, grace and gifts. When Paul described the church as
His "body" and "fullness," Paul emphasized its significance within
God's purposes.

Thought for the Day: Thank God today that when you
accepted Christ, you were baptized by one Spirit into the
body of Christ, the church (1 Cor. 13:13a).

DEAD IN TRANSGRESSIONS AND SINS

And you were dead in your trespasses and sins, **2** in which you formerly walked according to the course of this world, according to the prince of the power of the air, of the spirit that is now working in the sons of disobedience. **3** Among them we too all formerly lived in the lusts of our flesh, indulging the desires of the flesh and of the mind, and were by nature children of wrath, even as the rest.—**Eph. 2:1–3**

In this section for today, Paul reminded his readers of the mighty change that had taken place in their lives. He used the adjective **dead** figuratively to describe the state of being lost spiritually. This state is sometimes called *spiritual death.* The world, the devil and the flesh had previously directed their lives. Paul described this spiritual condition in three ways:

- walked according to the course of this world   v. 2
- walked according to the prince of   v. 2
  the power of the air
- lived in the lusts of their flesh, following its desires   v. 3

In verse 2, Paul used the term **walked** metaphorically to refer to their daily conduct or lifestyle. **World** refers to the satanically organized system that hates and opposes God.

The **prince of the power of the air** is the devil or Evil One (6:16). The *power of the air* is another way of saying the "heavenly realm," a term used in 6:12.

Paul characterizes the devil as the **spirit that is now working in the sons of disobedience** (v. 2). The devil uses supernatural power to exert a strong and compelling influence over the lives of lost men and women.

we too all formerly lived in the lusts of our flesh

In verse 3, Paul used *flesh* to refer to unregenerate humanity in its sinfulness and rebellion against God. Paul noted that prior to conversion, he and other Jewish believers exhibited conduct directly related to their unregenerate spiritual condition. Therefore, their thoughts and their actions were corrupt.

Because they were dead spiritually, they stood condemned before God, whose **wrath** upon them was imminent.

Thought for the Day: Thank God that you are no longer dead in your transgressions and sin, but have been made alive in Christ (2:5).

Notes:

_____

_____

_____

_____

_____

_____

GOD MADE YOU ALIVE WITH CHRIST

But God, being rich in mercy, because of His great love with which He loved us, 5 even when we were dead in our transgressions, made us alive together with Christ (by grace you have been saved)—**Eph. 2:4–5**

Paul described in verses 4–5 the gracious act of God in redeeming people from their desperate spiritual condition.

God, being rich in mercy describes His character and reveals *mercy* as one of His attributes. Because God is rich in mercy, He has an infinite amount of compassion on sinners suffering the calamity of sin. Paul cited **love** as another motivation for God's initiative in saving His people.

And you were dead in your trespasses and sins, is a clause Paul also used in verse 1 to explain his readers' previous condition as a state of death. Thankfully, now his readers have been made alive together with Christ. Paul's use of the pronoun "we" probably indicates that Jews along with Gentiles are now included among those who were spiritually dead but since then God "made us alive together with Christ." In verse 5, Paul made a sharp, direct contrast between their former condition outside Christ ("dead") and their present condition of being "made alive together with Christ."

In the parentheses Paul reminded his readers what God has done for them—saved them by His *grace*. The theological concept of grace stands opposed to any notion of work or merit to obtain salvation. Jesus' excruciating death vividly reveals God's great grace.

In summary, out of God's great mercy and love (v. 4) and grace (v. 5), He made Gentiles and Jews "alive together with Christ."

Thought for the Day: Praise God today that by His infinite mercy and great love, you have been saved by His grace.

GOD RAISED YOU UP WITH CHRIST

*And raised us up with Him, and seated us with Him in the heavenly places in Christ Jesus—***Eph. 2:6**

Yesterday we reflected on the fact that God made us spiritually alive with Christ (v. 5). Today we consider the gracious act of God in raising up Christians with Christ (v. 6). This shows a progression in God's actions towards believers.

Here Paul described God's saving actions more specifically. Believers have been **raised up with Him.** What God had accomplished in raising Christ (1:20) from the dead, He had also accomplished for the Ephesian believers through Christ. As Christ was raised *physically,* we were raised *spiritually.* Paul is referring to their *present* spiritual resurrection and not to their *future* physical bodily resurrection.

With the phrase, **seated us with Him in the heavenly places** Paul looked back to the exalted position of Christ, "far above all rule and authority and power and dominion" (1:21). This phrase informed his readers they *will* share in Christ's exaltation and victory over the powers (1:21; 2:1–2; 3:10; 6:10–20) when Christ returns. Then believers will be with Christ in the "heavenly places" or heavenly realms. At this time, believers being "in Christ," are seated in the heavenly places positionally or spiritually—but *not* literally. This spiritual position gives the believer the heavenly power to overcome the power of sin and death.

Thought for the Day: Praise God that by His salvation you have been made alive with Christ (v. 5), "raised" with Him, and "seated" with Him in the heavenly places (v. 6).

27

WHY DID GOD SAVE YOU?

So that in the ages to come He might show the surpassing riches of His grace in kindness toward us in Christ Jesus.—**Eph. 2:7**

Yesterday we considered how God "raised us up with Him and seated us with Him in the heavenly places" (v. 6). Today we will look at the *reason* God performed these two grace-oriented activities.

In verse 4, Paul noted that God's two attributes of rich *mercy* and great *love* motivated His saving initiative towards the readers. Here he gave another motivation for God to save the Ephesians—to demonstrate the "surpassing riches of His grace" toward wretched sinners. God gave this great grace to the Ephesians, and now to us, "in Christ Jesus."

The phrase, "in the ages to come" gives us the temporal setting for this manifestation of God's rich grace in humanity. You will note that "ages" is plural. This implies that one age follows immediately upon another. Therefore, we can interpret Paul's words as meaning that in all succeeding ages and throughout all eternity the society of saved sinners (church) is designed by God to reveal the "surpassing riches" of His divine goodness.

The last part of verse 7 describes God's entire work of salvation. The Greek word translated **kindness** denotes goodness or generosity. This is a striking statement because the recipients of His generosity had been God's enemies, liable to His wrath (v. 3).

In summary, God raises and exalts us mere mortals (v. 6) through Christ's death, resurrection and exaltation. Subsequently, He will "in the ages to come" continually display "the surpassing riches of His grace in kindness" that transformed us sinners (v. 7).

Thought for the Day: Reflect on the fact that God saved you to show the immeasurable wealth of His grace.

HOW IS ONE SAVED?

For by grace you have been saved through faith; and that not of
yourselves, it is the gift of God; **9** not as a result of works, so that
no one may boast.—**Eph. 2:8–9**

In these two verses, Paul informed his Gentile Christian readers
how they were saved. With the clause, **for by grace you have
been saved** Paul elaborated on the nature of God's salvation by
using two key theological terms—*grace* and *faith*. Grace is the basis
of salvation.

The phrase **through faith** is associated with "by grace." Faith is
the *means* by which salvation is appropriated by the sinner. Faith
itself cannot be a meritorious work, but rather the human response
by which one receives salvation that was accomplished in Christ
Jesus. The context (1:7; 2:5) of "through faith" indicates that Jesus is
the One to whom faith is directed. Thus, lost sinners must place their
faith in Jesus, not in their pastor, church membership, or any other
entity. To further emphasize the means of salvation, Paul added two
balancing negative clauses.

That not of yourselves, it is the gift of God emphasizes God's
initiative and activity in salvation. Consequently, the sinner's
response of faith does not come from any human source. Salvation
neither originates in nor is accomplished by the readers—it is God's
gift. Paul's clause, **not as a result of works**, so no one may boast
clearly indicates that salvation is not a reward for good deeds.
Therefore, **no one may boast** about his or her salvation.

Two key truths regarding salvation are found in this passage.
First, mankind cannot save itself by any kind of works. Second,
salvation comes from God on the basis of faith and therefore
excludes any human "boasting."

Thought for the Day: Today praise God for the greatest gift
ever given—God's salvation in Christ.

WHAT WAS GOD'S GOAL IN SAVING YOU?

For we are His workmanship, created in Christ Jesus for good works, which God prepared beforehand so that we would walk in them.—Eph. 2:10

In this verse Paul explained God's *goal* in saving the lost. His purpose was to create one new humanity out of Jews and Gentiles (Eph. 2:15).

The Greek noun translated **workmanship** stresses what believers have become because of God's grace working in them. Paul used it metaphorically to refer to God's *new creation*.

In this verse, we see two creation terms—*workmanship* and *created*. The Greek verb translated "created" means to make something that has not previously existed.

The phrase **in Christ Jesus** signifies our union with Christ Jesus. The new creation has been inaugurated by God through Jesus.

The phrase, **for good works** tells us God's *purpose* for His new creation. Good works is a general and comprehensive expression for godly behavior. As Christians, we have been created in Christ Jesus for the purpose of *good works*. Regarding works James stated: "For just as the body without the spirit is dead, so also faith without works is dead" (James 2:26). Here God emphasized the importance He places on "good works" in the lives of His new creations.

In summary, before the creation of the world, God **prepared** good works for His created workmanship (believers). He will perform these "good works" in and through them as they "walk" by faith in the power of the Holy Spirit.

Thought for the Day: With the help of His Holy Spirit, demonstrate a changed life style as you allow Him to render your attitudes and behavior more like Christ's. Remember, "faith without works is dead" (James 2:26).

THEN ... BUT NOW!

Therefore remember that formerly you, the Gentiles in the flesh, who are called "Uncircumcision" by the so-called "Circumcision," which is performed in the flesh by human hands— 12 remember that you were at that time separate from Christ, excluded from the commonwealth of Israel, and strangers to the covenants of promise, having no hope and without God in the world. 13 But now in Christ Jesus you who formerly were far off have been brought near by the blood of Christ.—**Eph. 2:11–13**

The *then-now* theme appears in this passage as it did in 2:1–6. The phrase **in the flesh** reminded his readers circumcision was an external act and consequently did not affect the heart.

The Jewish custom of **circumcision** was sufficiently distinctive in the first century for the Gentiles to be called **uncircumcision** by the Jews. Jews believed that the uncircumcised state of Gentiles was evidence of their estrangement from God.

The clause **performed in the flesh by human hands** stresses the human origin of circumcision and therefore stands in contrast to *God's* cleansing and recreating work in a person's heart.

Paul gave five deficiencies of the Ephesian believers before they were saved:

1. They were separated from Christ and on their way to hell.

2. They were excluded from the commonwealth of Israel. Previously they were outside God's election and isolated from a covenant relationship with Him.

3. They were "strangers to the covenants of promise." As Gentiles, they were excluded from the benefits of the old covenant.

4. They had "no hope." Only Christ's presence in the lives of Gentiles could produce eternal hope.

5. They were "without God." They had no covenant relationship with the true God.

In verse 13, Paul used the metaphors of **brought near** and **far off** to describe the contrast in their spiritual condition before and after accepting Christ. Having been *brought near* means they now have access to God and have been reconciled to God. *Far off* provides a picture of their spiritual state before accepting Christ. As pagan Gentiles, they had been far away from God's covenant promises.

Thought for the Day: Have you been "brought near" to God through Christ's shed blood on Calvary's cross?

Notes:

_____

_____

_____

_____

_____

_____

JESUS BROKE DOWN THE DIVIDING WALL

For He Himself is our peace, who made both groups into one and
broke down the barrier of the dividing wall—**Eph. 2:14**

Before Christ's death, burial and resurrection, there was a deep rift between the Jews and Gentiles. However, we learn that Christ broke down the dividing wall between these two groups and molded them into one new group.

Peace is the key theme in verses 14–18. Peace indicates a lack of hostility and a mutual acceptance between those who were previously hostile—Jews and Gentiles. In its broadest sense, peace denotes well-being, including salvation. Here, Paul equated Jesus with peace. **Our** refers to all believers, both Jews and Gentiles. The clause **who made both groups into one** refers to the resulting *unity* of Jewish and Gentile Christians.

The **dividing wall** Paul referred to was a literal wall in the temple in Jerusalem. The temple consisted of a series of five courts—the Court of the Gentiles, the Court of Women, the Court of the Israelites, the Court of the Priests and finally the Holy Place. A Gentile could only go as far as the Court of the Gentiles. This dividing wall was located between the Court of the Gentiles and the Court of Women. It was constructed of marble and was three cubits tall (approximately 4.5 feet).

This dividing wall separated the Gentiles from the *presence of God*. If a Gentile proceeded beyond this wall, he/she was liable to instant death. This wall was still standing when Paul wrote Ephesians.

Thought for the Day: Thank God today that He sent His Son so that *whoever* believes in Him will not perish but have eternal life (John 3:16). Further, praise God that as a Gentile you are not shut out from God's presence as Gentiles were before Christ's death.

JESUS ABOLISHED THE ENMITY

By abolishing in His flesh the enmity, which is the law of commandments contained in ordinances, so that in Himself He might make the two into one new man, thus establishing peace—Eph. 2:15

Today we will consider Jesus' purpose for removing this enmity by abolishing in His flesh the law (old covenant).

This wall in the temple can be considered the outward expression of **the law of commandments contained in ordinances**. By His death on the cross, Christ did not abolish *all* the Mosaic law. The moral law, primarily the Ten Commandments, are still in effect for Christians. The entire Mosaic law (moral, civil, and ceremonial) was the key component of the old covenant with Israel. However, with His death and resurrection, Jesus established a new covenant—a covenant with *all* people. With the new covenant, the Mosaic law and the old covenant were abolished and the barrier between Jews and Gentiles was removed.

The purpose of Jesus removing this **enmity** is twofold. We will discuss Jesus' second reason tomorrow. Today we'll consider the first: He did this to create in Himself one new man out of the two. Once the old covenant was abolished, there was no barrier to keep the two divisions of humanity apart. By His death, Jesus brought them together spiritually into a new creation—**one new man** or new creation in Christ. This one new man is a corporate entity—the people of Christ (Jews and Gentiles) whom Jesus created in Himself.

The theological basis for **peace** between two groups is peace with God. Consequently, only as Jews and Gentiles experience peace with God can they enjoy peace with each other.

Thought for the Day: Praise God today that you are living in the new covenant time period, the time of the "one new man"—the church.

JESUS RECONCILED BOTH TO GOD

And might reconcile them both in one body to God through the cross, by it having put to death the enmity.—**Eph. 2:16**

Yesterday we reflected on Jesus' first purpose for abolishing the enmity between Jews and Gentiles. Today we will reflect on Jesus' second purpose for abolishing the enmity.

Jesus' second purpose for abolishing the enmity was to **reconcile** the Jews and Gentiles to Himself. "Reconciliation" is an objective event that is accomplished by God for man's salvation. In this work of reconciliation to God, we see an emphasis on the *vertical* or Godward dimension in relationships. However, Paul did not drop the horizontal dimension completely from reconciliation because he specified how God reconciled them to God—**in one body**, which refers to the relationship of Jews and Gentiles.

Paul presented several truths in this verse. First, Jesus performs the reconciling to God. However, God both initiated and in Christ accomplished reconciliation. Second, God is the one to whom the two parties are reconciled. Third, "in one body" refers to the church, the body of Christ. In verse 15, Paul used the term "one new man" to communicate the concept of the church.

The phrase **through the cross** reaffirms the fact that the cross of Christ is the only ground for reconciliation to God.

By His death, Jesus **put to death the enmity** in two realms. First, He destroyed the enmity Jews and Gentiles experienced toward God (v. 16a). Second, He put to death the extensive rift between the Jews and Gentiles (v. 16b).

Thought for the Day: Today, thank God that Christ's death and resurrection broke down the enmity between the Jews and Gentiles

CHRIST PREACHED PEACE TO TWO GROUPS

AND HE CAME AND PREACHED PEACE TO YOU WHO WERE
FAR AWAY AND PEACE TO THOSE WHO WERE NEAR; **18** for
through Him we both have our access in one Spirit to the
Father.—**Eph. 2:17–18**

Paul noted **He came and preached peace.** Paul was probably referring primarily to Jesus although he could also have had in mind the apostles preaching later about the resurrected and exalted Christ. This *peace* resulted from Christ's sacrificial death on the cross.

Paul continued his theme of both the Jews and Gentiles being reconciled to God through Christ. The metaphor of **near** and **far away** has its roots in the OT. In Isaiah 57:19, we read of God's blessing on Jews in the land (those *near)* and His blessing on Jews that had been dispersed from Israel (those *far away*). Here Paul viewed the "near" and "far away" in light of Christ's fulfillment of OT prophecy. Christ brings messianic *peace* to both Jew and Gentile Christians.

In verse 18 Paul informed his readers of the *result* of Christ's work of reconciliation and His preaching of peace—**access** to God the Father. Now both Gentiles and Jews have access to God's presence. Before his conversion, Paul's concept of access to God was severely limited to the OT context of bringing sacrifices and offerings to the Lord (Lev. 1:3; 3:3; 4:14). However, *now* the access of both Jews and Gentiles to God is **through Him** (Christ)—not through priests and their sacrifices offered at the temple.

Paul's phrase, **in one Spirit** stresses the oneness of Jews and Gentiles in the church. In this verse, all three persons of the Trinity are involved in the believer's *access* to God.

Thought for the Day: Thank God today for the fact that as a Christian, you are a part of the family of God, whether you are a Jew or Gentile.

NO LONGER STRANGERS AND ALIENS!

*So then you are no longer strangers and aliens, but you
are fellow citizens with the saints, and are of God's
household—Eph. 2:19*

A **stranger** is someone allowed to be in a country but with no rights except those negotiated by treaty. **Aliens** are persons temporarily living in a land that is not theirs. Strangers and aliens are not citizens nor do they have the privileges citizens enjoy. Paul used these two images to describe the former spiritual status of his Gentile readers.

Specifically, the terms *strangers* and *aliens* probably refer to the Gentiles' previous relationship to God's people, Israel. In 2:11–12, Paul contrasted the previously lost condition of the Gentile Ephesians to the Jews' spiritual heritage—"excluded from the commonwealth of Israel, and strangers to the covenants of promise" (v. 12b). As pagan Gentiles, they did not have the covenants God made with Abraham, Moses and David.

However, Christ's work of reconciliation drastically changed their former spiritual condition from Gentile pagans to **fellow citizens with the saints** (Christians). This phrase stresses the Ephesians' spiritual unity with all believers, Jews and Gentiles.

Because the Ephesian Gentiles are now Christians, they have a homeland or commonwealth (v. 12b). In this verse, Paul's imagery moved to that of an intimate family—**God's household**. Gentile believers are members of the family of God; therefore some versions read, "members of God's household" (v. 19). In the Roman world of Paul's day, to be a member of a household meant *refuge, protection, identity* and provided *security* and a sense of belonging. The terms "household" and "citizens" are apt images for the church.

T **hought for the Day:** Thank God that as a Christian you are a member of God's household and experience His refuge and protection.

GOD'S TEMPLE IS BEING BUILT!

Having been built on the foundation of the apostles and prophets, Christ Jesus Himself being the corner stone, 21 in whom the whole building, being fitted together, is growing into a holy temple in the Lord, 22 in whom you also are being built together into a dwelling of God in the Spirit.—**Eph. 2:20–22**

The teaching and ministry of the twelve NT **apostles** (and Paul) and **prophets** serve as the foundation for the temple. Paul's Gentile readers had been built on Christ because He alone is the chief **cornerstone** of the building. In construction of that day, laying the cornerstone at the structure's base marked the beginning of the foundation. The foundation stones and all the other stones were determined by, or aligned with, the "cornerstone" (Christ). Further, the cornerstone unites the building because it is organically and structurally bound to the building.

Paul's construction imagery continued in verse 21 with **being fitted together** and is **growing into a holy temple**. *Being fitted together* refers to both the union of one stone with another and to the union of the structure with the cornerstone, Christ. "Being fitted together" and "growing into a holy temple" are ongoing activities, because the building is under construction.

The expression **a holy temple in the Lord** refers to the dwelling place of God as does the phrase, "a dwelling of God in the Spirit." The Jews and Gentiles have become the new temple, the place where God's presence dwells. Paul considered the "holy temple" to be God's people (the church) in whom He lives by His Spirit.

Thought for the Day: Praise God that because of Christ's reconciling work (v. 16) on your behalf you are a part of the church—in whom God dwells by His Holy Spirit.

38

THE MYSTERY OF CHRIST

For this reason, I, Paul, the prisoner of Christ Jesus for the sake of you Gentiles— **2** if indeed you have heard of the stewardship of God's grace which was given to me for you; **3** that by revelation there was made known to me the mystery, as I wrote before in brief. **4** By referring to this, when you read you can understand my insight into the mystery of Christ, **5** which in other generations was not made known to the sons of men, as it has now been revealed to His holy apostles and prophets in the Spirit; **6** to be specific, that the Gentiles are fellow heirs and fellow members of the body, and fellow partakers of the promise in Christ Jesus through the gospel—**Eph. 3:1–6**

Most scholars believe Paul wrote this epistle sometime during the two years he was imprisoned in Rome. The phrase **for the sake of you Gentiles** tells us the *reason* he is in prison. Because of Paul's ministry to the Gentiles, he spent a total of four years in prison.

Paul had not been in Ephesus for five or six years. Consequently, He reminded them of some facts he had taught them during his time in Ephesus. **The stewardship of God's grace** (v. 2) refers to the grace of God given to Paul so that he could make the **mystery of Christ** known (by preaching the word of God) to others, primarily the Gentiles. In verse 3 Paul reminded them *how* he became acquainted with the mystery—**by revelation** from God. When his readers were made aware of how the *mystery of Christ* was made known to him, Paul believed they would understand *why* he gained such great **insight into the mystery** (v. 4).

In previous **generations** (v. 5) Gentiles were kept apart from the Jews, by law and by culture. But during Paul's ministry, the mystery of Christ was being proclaimed to all peoples—Jews and Gentiles.

In verse 6, Paul reiterated the fact that Gentile Christians are:

- fellow heirs

- fellow members of the body of Christ

- fellow partakers of the promise in Christ Jesus.

Previously (2:12–16), Paul had mentioned some of these great spiritual blessings.

Thought for the Day: Praise God that He has made known the mystery of Christ to Jews and Gentiles.

Notes:

_____

_____

_____

_____

_____

_____

PAUL MADE A MINISTER OF THE GOSPEL

*Of which I am made a minister, according to the gift of God's grace which was given to me according to the working of His power. 8 To me, the very least of all saints, this grace was given, to preach to the Gentiles the unfathomable riches of Christ—***Eph. 3:7–8**

In verses 1–12, Paul discussed the ministry to which he had been called. In verse 7, he continued his emphasis on **God's grace** and turned his attention to how it related to his preaching to the Gentiles.

The phrase **according to the working of His power** is linked to the theme of God's *grace*. Paul experienced God's *enabling power* (grace) to carry out his apostleship to the Gentiles. In his trials, Paul experienced God's ongoing working of mighty power in all areas of life—spiritual, emotional and physical.

In verse 8, as Paul reflected on the commission he was given to be Christ's missionary to the Gentiles, he became deeply aware of his unworthiness to receive God's *grace*. When he created a Greek word **(the very least)**, Paul probably was thinking of how he had violently persecuted Christ's church. Specifically, God's **grace was given** to Paul to enable him to: (1) preach to the Gentiles the unfathomable riches of Christ, and (2) explain the mystery which for ages had been hidden in God (3:9).

This grace was *effective* and amazing because it enabled him to fulfill the demanding and sometimes dangerous missionary commission God gave him. The **unfathomable riches** refer to the wealth of divine grace and glory found in Christ and His gospel.

Thought for the Day: Thank God that as a believer, Jew or Gentile, you receive God's *grace* (divine enablement) and power daily to enable you to live for Christ.

PAUL BRINGS TO LIGHT THE MYSTERY

And to bring to light what is the administration of the mystery which for ages has been hidden in God who created all things
—Eph. 3:9

Yesterday we considered that God gave Paul grace and power to preach the unsearchable riches of Christ to the Gentiles. Today we will learn God also gave Paul grace (divine enablement) to bring to light the administration or plan of the mystery.

In 3:2, Paul mentioned the stewardship or administration of God's grace. There stewardship refers to the grace of God given to Paul to make the mystery known, primarily to the Gentiles. Paul's use of **administration of the mystery** (v. 9) is another way of expressing the *strategy* or plan of communicating the mystery. In verses 2 and 9 we see that God gave Paul the role of making the mystery known (**to bring to light**) to human beings on earth—both Jews and Gentiles.

God is now putting into effect His age-old plan (mystery) that was not previously seen or imagined by mankind. This **mystery** (that God would redeem His people and reconcile them to Himself through Christ's death) was **hidden in God**, Who had planned it before the foundations of the world (1:4). Therefore, salvation and the unity of Jew and Gentile in Christ have *always* been God's long range purpose.

The *goal* of God, who created all things, was to complete His work of spiritual recreation of mankind on the final day when He will bring all things together in unity in His Son (1:10).

Thought for the Day: Praise God that at the second coming of Christ you will receive your glorified body and your spiritual "recreation" will be complete.

PAUL'S PREACHING AND UNVEILING THE MYSTERY

So that the manifold wisdom of God might now be made known
through the church to the rulers and authorities in the heavenly
places. **11** This was in accordance with the eternal purpose which
He carried out in Christ Jesus our Lord, **12** in whom we have
boldness and confident access through faith in Him. **13** Therefore
I ask you not to lose heart at my tribulations on your behalf, for
they are your glory.—**Eph. 3:10–13**

Paul used **manifold** (v. 10) to speak of the diversified nature of divine wisdom. This **wisdom** works in diverse ways to unify Jews and Gentiles into one new person in Christ.

Paul informed his readers that God uses the church to enlighten the **rulers and authorities in the heavenly places** (v. 10) of His "manifold wisdom." The existence of Jews and Gentiles united into one body, the church, must be acknowledged by the powers. Consequently, the church becomes a graphic display of the multifaceted "wisdom of God." The *rulers and authorities* probably include the entire host of heavenly beings, good and evil. These evil powers cannot stop the spread of the gospel on earth.

God's intention or **eternal purpose** (v. 11) from all eternity was to, through the church, make known His many-splendored wisdom to the rulers and authorities in the heavenly realms.

Because believers are united with Christ they receive **boldness** and **confident access** to God that cannot be hindered by the hostile powers and authorities (v. 12). Therefore, Paul urged his readers not to become discouraged because of his sufferings (his imprisonment) on their behalf. Instead, his "tribulations" for declaring the "mystery" to them would result in their final, eternal glory (v. 13).

Thought for the Day: As a believer, do you regularly thank God for your ability to come boldly before His throne of grace (Heb. 4:16)?

INTRODUCTION TO PAUL'S SECOND PRAYER

For this reason I bow my knees before the Father, **15** from
whom every family in heaven and on earth derives its
name—**Eph. 3:14–15**

Paul's first prayer is recorded in 1:15–23. In verse 1 of this chapter Paul started to pray ("For this reason I...") for the Ephesians, but then digressed. Here, Paul resumed the prayer he began in verse 1. These two verses can be considered the introduction of Paul's prayer.

Paul prostrated himself (**bow my knees**) before God. This posture shows considerable reverence and submission. Intercession for his readers flowed out of his God-given ministry to the Gentiles. The term **Father** in the ancient world was a term of intimacy and possessed overtones of dignity and authority.

The word **family** stands for any group derived from a single ancestor. God is still naming every family in heaven and on earth, because He is still creating them. "Every family in heaven" points to family groupings and classes of angels (1:21), both good and rebellious because they owe their origin to God. "Every family on earth" probably refers to *earthly* family groupings.

In ancient times, a **name** was the means of revealing a person's true nature. Consequently, for God to give creatures a name signifies that He: (1) brought all creatures into existence; (2) exercises dominion over them; and (3) gives each its appropriate role.

In verse 15, Paul stressed God's sovereign power and authority in both heaven and on earth. Because some readers probably feared the threat of hostile powers (1:21), this verse would reassure them God is able to answer the petitions Paul verbalized in verses 16–19.

Thought for the Day: Praise God today that, like Paul, you can address God as Father. Also thank Him for His sovereign authority over all creatures in heaven and on earth.

FIRST PETITION IN PAUL'S PRAYER

That He would grant you, according to the riches of His glory, to be strengthened with power through His Spirit in the inner man, **17** so that Christ may dwell in your hearts through faith—**Eph. 3:16–17**

Paul petitioned God to give his readers *power.* The phrase **according to the riches of His glory** indicates the standard of God's giving—immeasurable and inexhaustible. Thus, Paul assured his readers the Father is able to meet their needs.

Paul used two different words for "power" in this prayer— **strengthen** and **with power.** Also, Paul prayed that God would empower the Ephesians "through His Spirit." The Holy Spirit and *power* are linked in other NT Scriptural passages. The **inner man** describes the place where the strengthening is to occur—the seat of personal consciousness.

So Christ may dwell in your hearts through faith explains how readers may be strengthened inwardly through the Holy Spirit. *In your hearts* is equivalent to "in the inner man" (v. 16). To "be strengthened with power... in the inner man" means that Christ dwells in the hearts of the readers. The focus of this request is not on the initial indwelling of Christ at conversion but on Christ's continued presence in their hearts. The Greek verb *dwell* is composed of two words, "to dwell" and "down deep" and means a deep indwelling of Christ down in the human heart.

"Heart" refers to the center of personality, thoughts, will, and emotions. Therefore, when Christ takes up residence in a person's heart, He is at the center of that person's life. "Through faith" informed Paul's readers that Christ's deep indwelling results from trusting Christ *daily* for salvation.

Thought for the Day: Have you let Christ become the controlling factor In your daily attitudes and conduct?

PAUL'S SECOND PETITION

And that you, being rooted and grounded in love, **18** may be able to comprehend with all the saints what is the breadth and length and height and depth, **19** and to know the love of Christ which surpasses knowledge, that you may be filled up to all the fullness of God.—**Eph. 3:17b–19**

Paul's second petition builds upon his first. In verse 17b, Paul shifted metaphors from **dwell** to **rooted** and **grounded.** The participial clause of verse 17b is grounded upon Paul's two previous infinitives: *strengthen* (v. 16) and *dwell* (v. 17a). As his readers are "strengthened" in the inner person by the Holy Spirit and Christ is "dwelling" deep down in their hearts, they can be established in love and comprehend the magnitude (*breadth, length, height* and *depth*) of Christ's love (v. 18).

Paul began his petition in verse 18. The four dimensions can be regarded as a unity. The **love of Christ** (v. 19a) is probably the object of this phrase. Then, Paul asked God to give them this power necessary to grasp the dimensions of Christ's love. The comprehension Paul requested is not merely intellectual reflection but is a personal knowledge. Paul wanted them individually to be empowered by God to understand the magnitude (dimensions) of Christ's love.

Surpassing knowledge indicates this love is so great one can never know it fully while earthbound. This knowledge is a true insight from God and is for the benefit of all believers. With this knowledge of Christ's love, His readers would become all that God wanted them to be—spiritually mature Christians.

Thought for the Day: Has God given you some insight into Christ's love for you?

DOXOLOGY TO PAUL'S SECOND PRAYER

Now to Him who is able to do far more abundantly beyond all that
we ask or think, according to the power that works within us, **21** to
Him be the glory in the church and in Christ Jesus to all generations
forever and ever. Amen—**Eph. 3:20–21**

Today we study the doxology to Paul's prayer. The doxology begins with an ascription of praise to God. In verse 20, Paul used three Greek words for divine power—**is able**, the **power** and **works** within us. God is able to accomplish incredibly great wonders on behalf of His people. These wonders are infinitely more than we ask or imagine. The adverb **far more abundantly** is best translated, "infinitely more than." Because God is infinitely powerful, there is no limit to what He can do.

Power refers to His capability to complete the task. The present participle **working** is from the Greek noun that gives us our English word energy. It is best to interpret it as "working," because the present tense emphasizes repeated action.

To give God glory (v. 21) involves actively acknowledging who He is or what He has done. With the phrase **in the church and in Christ Jesus** Paul told his readers where God is to be praised. The church is the epitome of God's grace. Believers can ascribe glory to God because they are "in Christ Jesus."

The prepositional phrase, **to all generations forever and ever** is a temporal phrase in which there is a mixture of time and eternity. **Glory** is due to God both for generations to come and throughout eternity. Paul used "Amen" to confirm what has been said. It could be translated, "let it be" or "truly."

Thought for the Day: Are you giving glory to God daily?

WALK IN A WORTHY MANNER

*Therefore I, the prisoner of the Lord, implore you to walk in a manner worthy of the calling with which you have been called—***Eph. 4:1**

This verse marks the dividing point in this epistle. In the first three chapters, Paul explained God's eternal plan to save mankind, the plan or "mystery" that had for ages been hidden in God (3:9). In the final three chapters, Paul gave a series of exhortations regarding how they should live ("walk").

In his eulogy (1:3–14), Paul praised God the Father (vv. 3–6), the Son (vv. 7–12), and the Holy Spirit (vv. 13–14). Paul reminded his readers that God **blessed us with every spiritual blessing...in** Christ (v. 3). Paul then presented specific blessings that God had bestowed upon them including:

- chose them in Christ   v. 4

- predestined them to adoption as sons through   v. 5
  Jesus Christ
- redeemed them through Christ's blood   v. 7

- forgave their sins   v. 7

- lavished His grace on them   v. 8

- provided them a heavenly inheritance   v. 11

Later Paul mentioned the ministry of the Holy Spirit and instructed his readers that the Spirit:

- sealed them in Him   v. 13

- was given to them as a pledge of their heavenly   v. 14
  inheritance

In 2:1–3 Paul elaborated on the mighty change that had taken place in their lives following their conversion. Later in this chapter, Paul specifically mentioned:

- God made them alive together with Christ   v. 5

- God raised them up spiritually   v. 6

- God saved them by His grace through faith   v. 8

- They are God's workmanship   v. 10
  (what God created in Jesus)

- Jesus removed the enmity between   vv.14–18
  Jews and Gentiles

Paul's allusion to being **the prisoner of the Lord** can have a dual purpose. First, it makes his following exhortations especially personal and urgent. Second, it reminded his readers of the price paid for discipleship.

Paul exhorted his readers to **walk** in a worthy manner. He had already used this metaphor to describe the readers' former lifestyle in sin and death (2:1–2). Later, by contrast, Paul used it in relation to the good works God had prepared for them to walk in (v. 10).

God's **calling** is a key concept in this context. Some aspects of God's calling include:

- it is the decision and action of God

- God's specific favor directed towards a people or person

- involves appointment to, and equipping for, a task to be fulfilled

- those called possess no worthiness of their own but are deemed worthy by God

It can be seen that God's call entrusts men and women with a high status and a correspondingly high responsibility and great task.

Paul's exhortation to **walk in a manner worth of the calling** is based on all the blessings which they were given when God saved them (chapters 1–3). This general exhortation serves as the basis for the rest of his epistle. His subsequent exhortations are amplifications of what is meant by—"walk in a manner worthy of the calling with which you have been called."

Thought for the Day: Are you walking daily in a manner that is worthy of God's high calling in Christ?

TWO CHARACTERISTICS OF THE BELIEVER'S WALK

With all humility and gentleness, with patience, showing tolerance
for one another in love—**Eph. 4:2**

Yesterday we reflected on walking worthily of one's calling in Christ Jesus. This is a broad exhortation that includes every aspect of our lives. Today we look at two specific characteristics of this "walk."

Paul listed four *graces* or behaviors (humility, gentleness, patience and tolerance) that should characterize the believer. It is significant the first grace Paul specified is **humility**. It was not considered a virtue by most people in ancient times. Consequently, a Greek word for humility did not exist before NT times.

Previously, Paul emphasized the unity of Jews and Gentiles into one body (2:16). In verses 3–6 of this chapter, Paul dealt with the unity of the church. *Humility* promotes unity while pride provokes disunity. Our supreme pattern for humility is Jesus, who was "meek and lowly in heart" (Matt. 11:29).

Humility and **gentleness** are closely associated. A synonym for gentleness is *meekness*. Jesus, who obtained salvation without use of force, was the epitome of gentleness.

Meekness is to characterize the lives of Christians as they relate to fellow believers. Gentleness or meekness involves considering the needs and feelings of others and results in willingness to waive one's rights. Meekness implies the conscious exercise of self-control, exhibiting gentleness toward others as opposed to using power to retaliate.

Thought for the Day: In Philippians we read, "Do nothing from selfishness or empty conceit, but with humility of mind regard one another as more important than yourselves" (Phil. 2:3). How are you doing in this area of your walk?

TWO MORE CHARACTERISTICS
OF THE BELIEVER'S WALK

With all humility and gentleness, with patience, showing tolerance
for one another in love—**Eph. 4:2b**

Yesterday we looked at the first two graces that characterize the believer's daily walk. Today we consider Paul's third and fourth graces.

Patience is evident in a believer who is walking in conformity with his or her calling. Patience can be defined as "cautious endurance that does not abandon hope." A Christian who possesses this characteristic lives day to day in peace, without seeing immediate results. The believer who wishes to live more patiently must: (1) exert conscious effort to live in this way; and (2) hourly rely on the Holy Spirit's help.

Because of God's patience with us, we ought to apply these two practical steps as we relate to others.

Showing tolerance for one another is the fourth characteristic Paul listed. This requires the grace of God because all believers possess weaknesses, failures, shortcomings, and blind spots. Mutual forbearance is a practical application of patience.

"Showing tolerance for one another" springs from one source— God's **love**. In 3:17 Paul had prayed that his readers would be "rooted and grounded in love." Now he urged his readers to live out this request in a practical way. Consequently, believers are not to merely tolerate other Christians, they are to tolerate them "in love." Paul's qualification is critical because tolerance *without* love could result in *resentment* or anger.

Thought for the Day: By God's grace, are you daily bearing with other believers in love, despite their weaknesses or shortcomings?

PRESERVE THE UNITY OF THE SPIRIT

Being diligent to preserve the unity of the Spirit in the bond of peace.—**Eph. 4:3**

The four graces Paul listed in verse 2 are necessary to achieve the exhortation we consider today.

The **unity of the Spirit** was Paul's way to describe the church's unity. In the Greek, Paul's exhortation possesses haste and urgency. This unity and reconciliation have been achieved through Christ's death (2:14–18). Therefore, believers do *not achieve* the unity, but they are exhorted to maintain it (2:11–22). To **preserve** the unity means *to maintain* it visibly and therefore it will be evident for others to observe.

In the bond of peace tells us *how* to maintain the unity of the Spirit. Further, this phrase informs us that the bond is peace. Here, "peace" refers to peace among believers. *Bond* means that which binds together, like the fastening of garments. Paul, being chained as a prisoner of the Lord (4:1), wrote of the binding or chaining together of peace.

Some Christians believe "peace" is the *means* by which the readers maintain the unity of the Spirit and others think peace is the *bond* that maintains their unity. Regardless of the precise way we interpret this phrase, believers are to make every effort to maintain oneness in their local congregations and in relationships with believers in other churches.

The "bond of peace" is possible because Christ brought peace between two former enemies (Jews and Gentiles, 2:14–16). To live in a way that mars the unity of the Spirit is to spite the gracious reconciling work of Christ.

Thought for the Day: Are you maintaining the "unity of the Spirit" by the way you relate to other Christians?

THERE IS JUST ONE BODY,
ONE SPIRIT, AND ONE HOPE!

There is one body and one Spirit, just as also you were called in
one hope of your calling.—**Eph. 4:4**

Paul discussed seven elements of unity in the body in verses 4–
6. Each begins with the word *one*. Three of these elements
deal with the three persons of the Trinity.

Paul probably mentioned **one body** first because this was Paul's
primary concern. In this context, Paul was probably referring to the
universal church. However, all he said about the universal church
also applies to each local congregation.

The **one Spirit** element of unity refers to the Holy Spirit Whom
Paul mentioned in 2:18 and 22. The one Spirit, by His indwelling
activity (4:3), brings unity and cohesion to the body. By the Holy
Spirit, we are baptized into one body (1 Cor. 12:13). Just as there is
only one body, there is also only *one* Holy Spirit.

What did Paul mean by **one hope**? Hope for believers is not like
the world's "hope so" type of hope. In contrast, the believer's hope is
the certainty that God will deliver on what He has promised. The
hope of the gospel is eternity in heaven.

The unity element "one hope" springs from God's call. God's
calling of each individual finds its foundation in the fact that "God
chose us in Him before the foundation of the world" (1:4a). God's
calling becomes effective in each individual's life when he/she
responds to the gospel message, is redeemed, and becomes a new
creature in Christ (2 Cor. 5:17).

Thought for the Day: Are you living in expectancy of the
glorious hope of heaven that originated in your calling
(1:18)?

ONE LORD, ONE FAITH, ONE BAPTISM

One Lord, one faith, one baptism—**Eph. 4:5**

Yesterday we considered the Holy Spirit. Today we look at what Paul said about Jesus, the second person of the Trinity.

Lord was the title for *Yahweh* (Hebrew word for God the Father) in the OT. Jesus was called Lord by His disciples and others (Matt. 17:4; Mark 10:51; Luke 5:8). Also, Lord is a favorite title for Jesus in the epistles.

Because of the Lord Jesus Christ's death, burial and resurrection, we can experience **faith.** Here, Paul can be referring either to objective or subjective faith. *Objective* faith is the body of doctrinal truth believed by all Christians. Doctrinal examples include: salvation by grace through faith, the existence of hell, heaven, Satan, and the inspiration of Scripture. *Subjective* faith in Christ is exercised (Col. 2:6–7) at the time of salvation and throughout the remainder of the Christian life.

The **one baptism** could refer to water baptism, the Spirit's baptism, or baptism into Christ's death. All three possibilities speak of the believer's union with Christ. Baptism and unity are sometimes connected, as in Galatians 3:27 and 1 Corinthians 12:13. Consequently, it is most likely Paul was thinking of how Christians at the time of salvation are "baptized into one body" (1 Cor. 12:13). Paul told the Galatian believers that, "all of you who were baptized into Christ have clothed yourselves with Christ" (Gal. 3:27).

Because of our baptism by the Holy Spirit into one body, we Christians have spiritual union with Christ.

Thought for the Day: Thank God today that when you accepted Christ as your Savior, the Holy Spirit baptized you into the one, and only, body of Christ.

54

ONE GOD AND FATHER OF ALL

One God and Father of all who is over all and through all and
in all.—**Eph. 4:6**

Yesterday we looked at Jesus and the fact there is one faith and one baptism. Today we turn our attention to God the Father.

one God and Father of all

This is Paul's climax to his three triads. God the Father is the unifying factor in both the Old and New Testaments. With *Father of all*, Paul referred to all Christians, rather than all humanity. In the context of Ephesians, this interpretation is reasonable because Paul is thinking of *unity* (4:3, 13) within the body. In 1:3 Paul reminded his readers God is the Father of Christ. Subsequently, the Father of all those who are in Christ refers to Christians.

who is over all

With *who is over all*, Paul is emphasizing God's supreme *transcendence*—God's distinctiveness from and absolute sovereign superiority over His creation.

and through all and in all

Here Paul expressed God's *immanence*—the idea of God indwelling His entire universe and its processes. With the clause, "who is over all and through all and in all," Paul was referring to both God's transcendence and immanence. These two attributes of God comprise the basis for the unity of the Spirit (1:3), which believers are to maintain.

Thought for the Day: Remember that your Father is the Father of all believers. Therefore, your Father is asking you to be unified with **all** His children to whom you relate.

EACH BELIEVER HAS BEEN GIVEN GRACE

But to each one of us grace was given according to the measure of Christ's gift. 8 Therefore, it says, "WHEN HE ASCENDED ON HIGH, HE LED CAPTIVE A HOST OF CAPTIVES, AND HE GAVE GIFTS TO MEN." —**Eph. 4:7–8**

In verses 1–6 Paul presented the basis of unity. Now in verses 7–10, Paul emphasized the fact there is diversity in unity.

Each individual Christian receives **grace**, a particular divine enablement (spiritual gift) given to each believer to empower them for ministry. All believers receive at least one spiritual gift. The fact that different believers receive different gifts does not hurt the unity of the body. Instead, the various spiritual gifts enrich the whole body.

Paul tells us who gives the spiritual gifts—Jesus Christ. Christ distributes grace (spiritual gifts) in varied measure to each individual. Jesus also determines the *amount* of the gift (Rom. 12:3, 6–8).

In verse 8, Paul paraphrased Psalm 68:18. This psalm is a song of victory ("YOU HAVE LED CAPTIVE YOUR CAPTIVES") over foes. These "captives" could represent the powers of evil that He conquered at Calvary. "YOU HAVE ASCENDED ON HIGH" of Psalm 68:18a probably refers to Christ's exaltation (His resurrection and ascension, Acts 1:9). It appears Paul took the theme of **gifts to men** from Psalm 68:18 ("YOU HAVE RECEIVED GIFTS AMONG MEN") and applied it to the church at Ephesus. Christ gave men and women spiritual gifts.

Thought for the Day:. Thank God today that as Christ received spoils of war from His enemies (Ps. 68), He now gives gifts to those who are on His side—His children.

HE DESCENDED AND ASCENDED

(Now this expression, "He ascended," what does it mean except that He also had descended into the lower parts of the earth? 10 He who descended is Himself also He who ascended far above all the heavens, so that He might fill all things.)—**Eph. 4:9–10**

In verse 9, Paul here presented his readers with a rhetorical question to draw attention to the phrase "He ascended." Paul's clause, **He who ascended far above all the heavens** was his way of expressing Jesus' ascent into heaven some days after His resurrection (Acts 1:9).

By **He descended... into the lower parts of the earth** what time period is Paul referencing? Probably Christ's *descent* from heaven to earth at His incarnation and subsequently His death on the cross for us. With His death and resurrection, Jesus won the victory over Satan and sin.

The plural **heavens** indicates that a number of heavens, three, seven, or even more could be in view. Paul was telling his readers that Jesus had ascended above everything to the place of highest supremacy. "All the heavens" is a metaphorical reference to the "all rule and authority and power and dominion" which Paul mentioned in 1:21.

So that He might fill all things is a purpose clause for why He "ascended far above all the heavens." The verb "fill" signifies to control by exercising authority. Consequently, Jesus Christ fills all things (the universe) by exercising His lordship over everything. He is the powerful ruler over "all rule and authority and power and dominion" (1:21a).

Thought for the Day: Praise God that He sent Jesus to die for you ("descended into the lower parts of the earth") and resurrected Him enabling Jesus to win the victory over sin for you!

CHRIST GAVE MINISTERS TO THE CHURCH

And He gave some as apostles, and some as prophets, and some as evangelists, and some as pastors and teachers.—**Eph. 4:11**

Here Paul mentioned specific gifted persons Christ gives to the church. Paul is listing spiritual gifts given to Christians, not primarily offices in the church. These gifted persons enable the members of the church to function and develop as they should.

The four ministries of **apostles, prophets, evangelists,** . . . **pastors and teachers** within the body are universally needed and mutually shared. These gifted persons and their functions minister to the *entire* body of Christ.

Apostles were official delegates of Jesus Christ, commissioned to proclaim the message in oral and written form. Some believe the apostolic gift is still given today, though in a secondary way, possibly for the purpose of starting new churches.

Prophets. In the early NT church, prophecy was a gift of the Holy Spirit and was part of the worship experience, because prophets communicated divine revelation. Apostles and prophets provided the foundational role for the church because they served as the authoritative recipients and proclaimers of the mystery of Christ before the canon of Scripture was completed.

Evangelists were engaged in the preaching of the gospel. By their activity, they carried on the work of the apostles. Paul linked **pastors** and **teachers** which suggests their functions in the church overlapped. All pastors teach Scripture, but not all teachers are pastors. In NT times, teachers did not impart new revelation directly from the Lord, as did the prophets.

Thought for the Day: Thank the Lord today that He gifts people to minister in the church and He gives a spiritual gift to each believer—you are a "gifted" person!

PURPOSES OF GIVING GIFTED PERSONS

For the equipping of the saints for the work of service, to the building up of the body of Christ.—**Eph. 4:12**

Yesterday we considered four groups of gifted persons Christ gave to the church. Today we will discover two purposes for Christ giving these gifted individuals to His church.

Paul offered the immediate purpose for giving the gifted persons as—**equipping the saints for the work of service**. Equipping can also mean preparing, completing, training, or disciplining. God has given the church pastors, elders, teachers, prophets, and evangelists to prepare and equip the saints for their works of service. These special ministers function to make God's people qualified to minister to others, or as Paul said, "for the work of service."

"Work" here describes an ongoing activity on the part of individual believers as they "serve" others. The "work of service" on the part of individual believers corresponds to Paul's earlier statement, "to each one of us grace was given" (4:7a). Therefore, every believer must do the work of the ministry.

The second purpose of Christ giving gifted persons to the church was for the **building up the body of Christ**. Here Paul again used a metaphor—of building as he did in 2:21. "Building up" is used figuratively of the establishment and growth (2 Peter 3:18) of individual Christians. This in turn implies the development of the entire church (group of individuals).

In summary, the work of the ministry *by every believer* is for the purpose of building up Christ's body.

Thought for the Day: By God's grace are you using the spiritual gift Christ gave you to do the constant work of service to build up the body of Christ?

ATTAINING THE UNITY OF THE FAITH

Until we all attain to the unity of the faith, and of the knowledge of the Son of God, to a mature person, to the measure of the stature which belongs to the fullness of Christ. **—Eph. 4:13**

In verse 13, Paul gave three prepositional phrases to explain three aspects of the final goal of attaining maturity.

Unity among believers increases as their knowledge of the Son of God increases. This is true in individual and corporate (church) experience. Now as believers walking by faith we experience tension. Even though this faith has already been given to believers (4:5), its complete oneness is not yet fully achieved. The goal of attaining the unity of the faith will not be reached until Christ's second coming.

The phrase **to a mature person** in the Greek is literally, "into a perfect, full-grown man." The adjective *mature* means "having reached its end." The *singular* form *mature person* probably refers to the church (body of Christ) as a single entity, also referred to in the phrase "one new man" in Christ (2:15). As individual believers grow and contribute spiritual growth to the body, the body as a whole grows.

This third prepositional phrase refers to attaining full spiritual growth. This also could be written "attain to the **measure** which is Christ's full **stature**." If all Christians used their spiritual gifts regularly, the church would measure up to Christ's full stature. The goal to be reached is mature personhood. The extent of this spiritual growth is measured by "Christ's full stature." Paul expressed full spiritual maturity with the phrase "the fullness of Christ."

Thought for the Day: Praise God that He can help you grow spiritually and become a mature person, and thereby contribute to the spiritual growth of the entire body.

WE ARE NO LONGER TO BE CHILDREN

As a result, we are no longer to be children, tossed here and there
by waves and carried about by every wind of doctrine, by the
trickery of men, by craftiness in deceitful scheming.—**Eph. 4:14**

In verse 14, Paul continued his theme of maturity by contrasting the mature Christian (v. 13) against children. Paul associated himself with his readers by using **we**. By using the "children" metaphor, Paul was referring to their spiritual infancy. In describing some features of their spiritual infancy, Paul changed metaphors.

tossed here and there by waves

This metaphor of immature believers being like little *boats* on turbulent waters refers to *confusion*. The false doctrines these believers heard were like strong currents of wind ("every wind of doctrine") that stir up water into waves and endanger the little boats. Then, as now, religious philosophies threatened to undermine the gospel by confusing believers.

The noun **trickery** literally means "dice playing." It may have indicated the dice were loaded. Paul used the word metaphorically of a trickery that results from craftiness. Through their craftiness, the false teachers endeavored to *trick* believers.

Here **deceitful scheming** refers to *strategy*. The seductive cunning of the false teachers was organized. False teachers organized error for the goal of undermining the truth of God. Their "trickery" was calculated to lead others astray.

Thought for the Day: Thank God today that Jesus has given His gifts and gifted people to the church. As they help build up His body, the instability and immaturity of many believers will gradually decrease.

BUT SPEAK AND DO THE TRUTH IN LOVE

But speaking the truth in love, we are to grow up in all aspects
into Him who is the head, even Christ.—**Eph. 4:15**

This side of heaven, the goal Paul envisioned for the Ephesian believers was spiritual growth. It would result as they spoke the truth in love rather than being misled by the malicious scheming of false teachers.

Here the participle **speaking** means "truthing" or "doing the truth." Paul exhorted them to do more than speak honestly. The content of their testimony is to be "the word of truth, the gospel of your salvation" (1:13a). In addition, **truth** is part of the soldier's armor: "having girded your loins with truth" (6:14a).

A key phrase is **in love**. The truth they are to proclaim is not separated from love or proclaimed at the expense of love. Truth may be demonstrated harshly, but Paul asked that it be done "in love."

Paul was considering growth in a comprehensive way. He could have been thinking of such aspects as: in faith, in knowledge, in grace, in unity, in love, in development of proper attitudes, or in the exercise of spiritual gifts.

Christ is the *goal* of the growth of the body and the One into whom we are to grow. Here, the readers' maturity in Him is the goal. Again, Paul used "we" to show that he included himself among those who are progressing and maturing into Christ.

Christ is the **head** of the church (Col. 1:18; 2:19; Eph. 1:22, 23). The members of the body of Christ are dependent on the "head" to nourish and to unify them.

Thought for the Day: Ask God to help you continue to grow in all aspects into Him—in faith, in love, in grace, in your development of proper attitudes, and in your exercise of spiritual gifts.

62

THE GROWTH OF THE BODY

*From whom the whole body, being fitted and held together by
what every joint supplies, according to the proper working of each
individual part, causes the growth of the body for the building up
of itself in love.—Eph. 4:16*

From whom denotes the source of the growth of **the whole
body**. Christ, the head of the body, is the *source* (4:15). Here
Paul used the metaphor of the physical "body."

Paul also addressed the unique contribution each member ("each
individual part") may provide to the body's life and development.
Paul introduced a metaphor from the building trade here. **Being
fitted** in the Greek language comes from a verb meaning "to join," as
stones for a tomb. In Paul's day, masons did not use mortar, but cut
and smoothed each stone so it would fit exactly ("being fitted") with
each adjoining stone. This helped the stone wall hold together. In the
spiritual life, God's grace helps individual believers be "fitted and
held together" (grow together) which brings inner unity.

Paul continued the physical body metaphor with, **by what every
joint supplies**. Many parts of the physical body are held together by
joints. So this phrase could refer to the work of gifted ministers of
the Word helping individual Christians ("each individual part") grow
and later minister to others. The gifted ministers ("every joint")
provide connections and support between the other members of the
body.

Love is the key criterion for an accurate assessment of the
church's true growth. Only "in love" can Christian ministry be
effective and subsequently contribute to **building up** the body.

Thought for the Day: Are you growing spiritually and
contributing to the growth of the corporate "body," the
church?

DO NOT LIVE LIKE THE GENTILES!

So this I say, and affirm together with the Lord, that you walk no longer just as Gentiles also walk, in the futility of their mind, **18** being darkened in their understanding, excluded from the life of God because of the ignorance that is in them, because of the hardness of their heart; **19** and they, having become callous, have given themselves over to sensuality for the practice of every kind of impurity with greediness.—**Eph. 4:17–19**

Paul moved from the growth of the body to how individual Christians are not to walk. They are not to live or "walk" as the Gentiles live. Most believers in Ephesus were Gentiles, and many previously had a lifestyle similar to that of pagan Gentiles.

Paul used the phrase **in the futility of their mind** to inform his readers that pagan Gentiles did not know God. Further, they could not perceive God's revelation. It is futile to have good sound minds yet not be able to know and perceive God and His revelation.

Because pagan Gentiles were **darkened in their understanding,** their reasoning process was *darkened* or decreased. The **ignorance that is in them** refers to their ignorance of God's revelation and will. Because they are "excluded from the life of God," pagan Gentiles are separated from the life that comes only from God—spiritual life. In addition, they are "dead" in their trespasses and sins (2:1, 5).

The **hardness of their heart** toward God and their alienation from the "life of God" caused them to become insensitive ("callous") to God and His ways. Therefore they gave **themselves over to sensuality** and lived with no moral restraints.

Thought for the Day: Ask God to show you any areas where you are possibly "walking" as the pagan Gentiles walk.

YOU HAVE LEARNED, HEARD, AND BEEN TAUGHT IN JESUS

*But you did not learn Christ in this way, **21** if indeed you have heard Him and have been taught in Him, just as truth is in Jesus.*—**Eph. 4:20–21**

In verses 17–19, Paul exhorted his readers not to live or "walk" as the Gentiles walk. In today's passage, Paul reminded them of the teaching they had received.

At conversion, the Ephesians started to **learn** about Christ. After conversion, believers can and should continually learn more about Christ. The poor, non-Christ like conduct of pagan Gentiles is not what the Ephesian believers learned regarding Christ. Paul had spent eighteen months in Ephesus. No doubt he and his disciples regularly and extensively taught the new Ephesian converts.

The Ephesian believers did not hear Christ preach in person. Instead, they **heard** about Him in the gospel messages and teaching they received from Paul. Therefore, through hearing about Christ and His teachings, they learned about Christ.

have been taught in Him

Paul picked up on the point of ongoing instruction that had been given to the Ephesian believers.

In verse 20 Paul used Jesus' title, Christ; in verse 21 he used Jesus' *name*. Paul probably did this to stress that the historical Jesus is the embodiment or personification of **truth**. In John 14:6, Jesus said, "I am the way, and the *truth*, and the life; no one comes to the Father but through Me."

Thought for the Day: Are you applying on a daily basis the many teachings and truths of Christ?

PUT OFF THE OLD SELF!

That, in reference to your former manner of life, you lay aside the old self, which is being corrupted in accordance with the lusts of deceit.—**Eph. 4:22**

Here Paul gave his first exhortation regarding the process of spiritual growth sometimes called *progressive sanctification*. His exhortation is the first step of the process. The second step is being renewed in the spirit of your mind (v. 23), while the third step is to "put on" the new self (v. 24).

In verses 22 and 24, Paul used a clothing *metaphor*—**lay aside** and *put on*. With the term **old self**, Paul referred to the sin nature each Ephesian believer possessed and the resulting "former manner of life." The corrupt sin nature is personified as the "old self"— deformed, decrepit and tending to corruption. Paul exhorted his readers to "lay aside" these sinful actions and/or attitudes as one takes off ragged and filthy garments. Some of these sins include: anger, pride, greed, jealousy, selfishness, fornication, and envy.

Progressive sanctification results in a believer becoming increasingly separated from sin and becoming more like Christ. The process is a joint effort between Christians and God. Consequently, this process involves human responsibility and divine activity. Further, it can be accomplished only through the power and help of the Holy Spirit.

To successfully engage in this process, the believer must continually remember two truths. First, the believer must have a genuine desire to be progressively sanctified daily. Second, the believer relies on the Holy Spirit to: daily renew the mind and help "lay aside" sins and replace them with ("put on") godly virtues.

Thought for the Day: Are you daily asking God to help you "lay aside" sins of the flesh or the sin nature?

BE RENEWED IN THE SPIRIT OF YOUR MIND

And that you be renewed in the spirit of your mind. —**Eph. 4:23**

Yesterday we discussed the first step in *progressive sanctification*—"lay aside" the old self. Today we reflect on the second step—being **renewed in the spirit of your mind.**

Paul urged each believer to be *renewed* in the spirit of his or her mind. *Renewed* is a present tense participle. Therefore, Paul pictured this renewal as a process continuing throughout the believer's life.

Also, it is in the passive voice in the Greek language, suggesting that God is the One who effects the ongoing work of renewing minds. However, Paul's implied exhortation emphasized the continual challenge for each believer. Believers are to *yield themselves* to God (Rom. 6:13), which will enable them to be renewed by God in their inner persons. The process of "progressive sanctification" depends on the constant renewing of the minds of believers. Earlier, Paul noted that heathen degradation is due to the futility of their minds (4:17).

In a related passage, Paul exhorted Roman believers: "And do not be conformed to this world, but be transformed by the *renewing* of your mind, so that you may prove what the will of God is, that which is good and acceptable and perfect" (Rom. 12:2).

Reading, studying, and meditating on the Word are some primary means of allowing God to renew your mind. Regularly attending worship services and having consistent times of private prayer also help *renew* the spirit of the Christian's mind.

Thought for the Day: The mind is critical to living the Christian life. Are you getting into the Word daily and allowing the Holy Spirit to: convict, encourage, and transform you?

PUT ON THE NEW SELF

And put on the new self, which in the likeness of God has been created in righteousness and holiness of the truth. —**Eph. 4:24**

Progressive sanctification requires the believer to continually abandon sin ("lay aside the old self," v. 22), and be "renewed in the spirit of your mind" (v. 23). Today we consider the final step in progressive sanctification—put on the new self.

In verse 24 Paul again picked up the clothing *metaphor*—"put on." In the KJV it is rendered "new man." The new self is part of the new creation. In 2 Corinthians 5:17 Paul stated: "Therefore if anyone is in Christ, he is a *new creature*; the old things passed away; behold new things have come."

Because believers are part of God's new creation, their conduct should be consistent with their new position and status in Christ. As the new creation is put on, we must appropriate it through faith. *Divine activity* and *human responsibility* are balanced in this process of putting on the new self.

In putting on the new self, the believer daily supplements faith with godly practices and virtues such as:

- Humility, gentleness, patience, showing tolerance in love
- speaking truth, forgiving, and showing kindness.

These added practices and virtues constitute the "new self."

As with steps one and two, the believer can carry out the third step only with the help and power of the Holy Spirit.

Thought for the Day: Are you daily asking God to help you "put on" the new self by adding, with the Holy Spirit's help, virtues such as: humility, gentleness, patience, and forgiveness?

SPEAK THE TRUTH AND MANAGE YOUR ANGER

Therefore, laying aside falsehood, SPEAK TRUTH EACH ONE of you WITH HIS NEIGHBOR, for we are members of one another. **26** BE ANGRY, AND yet DO NOT SIN; do not let the sun go down on your anger, **27** and do not give the devil an opportunity.—**Eph. 4:25–27**

The exhortations Paul gave in verses 25-32 flowed from his exhortations in verses 22-24. In verses 25-32, Paul exhorted his readers to be actively involved in *progressive sanctification*.

While the "old self" was characterized by the *lusts of deceit* (v. 22b), believers who are "putting on" the new self will **lay aside falsehood.** Paul followed his negative command with a positive command—**speak truth each one of you with his neighbor.** The believer who is putting on the "new self" exhibits righteousness and holiness which are based on **truth** (vv. 24, 25). **For we are members of one another** is the motivating clause for Paul's positive exhortation. Deception by one member harms that member and the entire body suffers.

In verse 26, Paul taught that believers may become **angry,** but must not act out their anger sinfully. Because people have a tendency to allow anger to control them, the negative part of this command was needed. So believers would not allow anger to degenerate into sin, Paul set a strict time limit on it—before the sun goes down! This prevents believers from brooding in anger or nursing it. Paul directed his readers to deal with anger promptly by reconciling to the person as soon as possible.

Paul's third command (v. 27) regarding anger gave his readers the *motivation* for dealing with anger promptly. Anger can give **the devil an opportunity** to cause strife within the lives of individual believers and within the entire body.

Thought for the Day: Are you dealing promptly with your anger?

DO NOT STEAL!

He who steals must steal no longer; but rather he must labor,
performing with his own hands what is good, so that he will have
something to share with one who has need.—**Eph. 4:28**

Here Paul now addressed a third area of behavior that some readers needed to deal with if they were going to "lay aside the old self" (v. 22).

With the clause **he who steals must steal no longer**, some scholars believe Paul was referring to day laborers or skilled tradesmen whose work was seasonal. When laborers were out of work in that time there were no unemployment benefits for them. Consequently, some turned to stealing. Paul's negative command indicates Ephesian believers must have had difficulty breaking away from these ethical norms in their society.

Paul's negative command is followed with this positive exhortation—**but rather he must labor, performing with his hands what is good**. Because the believer is to lay aside stealing and "put on" work, all things are to be acquired with labor. "Good" denotes that which is beneficial to others in society. Also, working with one's hands is viewed as doing what is good.

so that he will have something to share with one

Paul presented his readers with a motivation for this positive command. The purpose for work is not self-indulgence, but to benefit those in need. Often those who benefit by this sharing are fellow needy believers.

Thought for the Day: Is there any way you are stealing from your employer? Examples could include breaks longer than allowed and using company time for personal phone conversations.

SPEAK IN AN EDIFYING MANNER

Let no unwholesome word proceed from your mouth, but only such a word as is good for edification according to the need of the moment, so that it will give grace to those who hear.—**Eph. 4:29**

Today we consider Paul's exhortation regarding a fourth area of behavior to *lay aside*—their unwholesome speech.

Paul's negative exhortation **let no unwholesome word proceed from your mouth** is rather comprehensive. Paul used the term "word" which is singular. Therefore, he meant not one single word the readers uttered should be harmful to others. Harmful, degrading speech defiles the speaker (Matt. 15:11) and is destructive to body life.

Then Paul gave his readers a positive command **but only such a word as is good for edification** regarding their speech. Beneficial words should be used for building up (*edification*) a needy member or a needy body of believers. This kind of speech will supply some deficiencies in the lives of other believers. As these deficiencies are met, the spiritual growth of the body will increase. Every believer will be accountable for each word spoken during one's lifetime.

So that it will give grace to those who hear is the motivation Paul presented for his positive command. As believers are progressively sanctified ("lay aside" unwholesome words and "put on" edifying words), they develop new, Christ like standards of speech. Then their words will be a blessing to others—even the means by which God's grace comes to hearers.

In summary, Paul exhorted his readers to "build up" other believers by speaking to them in edifying ways. What a privilege believers have in partnering with God to edify other believers!

Thought for the Day: Is your speech always positive and edifying? Or does it deteriorate under stressful or other negative circumstances?

DO NOT GRIEVE THE HOLY SPIRIT OF GOD

Do not grieve the Holy Spirit of God, by whom you were
sealed for the day of redemption.—**Eph. 4:30**

Today we look at a negative and sobering command Paul gave his readers. This exhortation applies in a general way to the results of poor conduct, rather than to a specific negative behavior such as stealing (v. 28). This negative imperative provided additional *motivation* to obey Paul's four previous exhortations regarding behavior.

Grieving the Holy Spirit can be the result of not abandoning sins daily and replacing them with Godly virtues. The *Holy Spirit of God* is the full title for the Holy Spirit that emphasizes:

- the identity of the One who may be offended and

- the seriousness of this sin.

Do not grieve is a present tense imperative verb, which describes action as an ongoing process. Therefore, the believer needs to continually avoid grieving the Holy Spirit.

Paul presented his readers with a thought-provoking motivation. By **sealing** believers with His Spirit, God has:

- stamped them with His character

- guaranteed to protect them until He takes final possession of them on the day of redemption

Therefore, believers who behave in ways that grieve the Holy Spirit, by whom they have been marked as God's own, are highly ungrateful. The *day of redemption* refers to the final day of salvation, also called the day of the Lord (1 Thess. 5:2; 1 Cor. 1:8; 5:5).

In relation to time, redemption can be viewed as having two phases. First, redemption sets us free from sin and its obligations while on earth. Second, the ultimate, complete redemption occurs at the second coming of Christ. At His second coming, Jesus sets believers free from the presence of sin.

On the final day of salvation, God will completely redeem His own possession. His followers will be completely redeemed because their glorified bodies will not have sin natures. God's guarantee of this truth is sealing them now with His Holy Spirit.

Thought for the Day: As you go about your activities, reflect on the seriousness of grieving the Holy Spirit.

Notes:

_____

_____

_____

_____

_____

_____

DO AWAY WITH ANGER, BITTERNESS, ETC.!

Let all bitterness and wrath and anger and clamor and
slander be put away from you, along with all malice. **32** Be
kind to one another, tender-hearted, forgiving each other,
just as God in Christ also has forgiven you.—**Eph. 4:31–32**

Bitterness may result when one has been wronged by another. Then an inner, resentful attitude may result. Consequently, bitterness deals primarily with attitude. It is harbored hatred for a person. **Wrath** refers to hot anger or passion. It is a more agitated condition of the feelings than anger. Wrath quickly flares up and quickly subsides. **Anger**—wrath expresses more the inward feeling. Anger is a more active emotion than wrath. Anger is a more settled condition of mind than wrath and frequently involves revenge. Wrath and anger deal with the disposition of one's temperament.

Clamor denotes an outcry, or speaking loudly (Acts 23:9). **Slander** consists of abusive speech. Clamor and slander deal with the *manner* of speech.

Being kind to others (v. 32) does not come naturally and cannot be produced from one's innate resources. Only as a believer relies on the Holy Spirit for help, is it possible to be *kind* to one another. Being "kind, tender-hearted" describes the lifestyle of showing *favor, kindness,* and *pleasantness* to others. As believers follow this pattern, they will be sympathetic to the needs of others.

"Just as God in Christ also has forgiven you" is the motivation Paul gave for his positive command. God's gracious act of giving Christ to purchase our redemption is a profound illustration of how believers are to relate to each other.

Thought for the Day: How are you relating to other believers in the body of Christ? Are you harboring anger or bitterness toward another believer?

IMITATE GOD AND WALK IN LOVE

Therefore be imitators of God, as beloved children; **2** and walk in love, just as Christ also loved you and gave Himself up for us, an offering and a sacrifice to God as a fragrant aroma.—**Eph. 5:1–2**

In this paragraph (4:25–5:2), Paul provided five exhortations regarding poor behavior in verses 26–32. Today we will look at the last two commands in this paragraph.

In verse 1, Paul used the present tense imperative "to become imitators" rather than "to be" (kind) as he did in 4:32. Therefore, Paul instructed his readers to be *imitating* God continuously.

The kind of **love** (v. 2) Paul was considering was God's love (*agape*). Agape love is given without regard to merit and seeks the other person's highest good. The supreme example of love was demonstrated by Christ giving Himself for us on a cruel cross.

Offering and sacrifice convey the idea that Christ handed Himself over to God as the offering and sacrifice to fulfill all the offerings and sacrifices of the OT. These two words placed together refer to sacrifice and their background is the OT sacrifices. By the term **fragrant aroma**, Paul was alluding to the OT sense of a sacrifice being *acceptable to God* (Isa. 56:7; Lev. 1:4: Phil. 4:18). Consequently, by using the term *fragrant aroma*, Paul stressed that Christ's sacrifice was completely acceptable to God.

The love Christ demonstrated by giving Himself up as an offering and sacrifice to God is to be imitated by Christians as we "walk in love." Our sacrificial love for other believers becomes a sacrifice *acceptable* to God.

Thought for the Day: Are you daily "walking in love?"

IMMORALITY, IMPURITY, AND GREED

But immorality or any impurity or greed must not even be named among you, as is proper among saints; **4** and there must be no filthiness and silly talk, or coarse jesting, which are not fitting, but rather giving of thanks.—**Eph. 5:3–4**

In a previous paragraph (4:17–24), Paul was contrasting the lifestyles of unbelievers and believers. In 5:3–4, Paul continued this contrast. He began by listing a terrible trio—sexual immorality, impurity, and greed. Immorality and impurity are two of the deeds of the flesh that are listed in Galatians 5:19.

Immorality denotes any kind of illegitimate sexual relationships especially adultery and sexual relations with prostitutes. **Impurity** means moral impurity that defiles the whole person, and subsequently affects every area of life. **Greed** is the root of immorality and impurity and can be defined as the insatiable desire to have more, even the coveting of someone else's body for selfish gratification.

All the forms of sexual immorality and greed are so serious Paul stated they are not even to be mentioned among God's people. The holiness (progressive sanctification) of his readers is both **proper** (v. 3b) and *essential*. Further, the lifestyle of all believers is to be consistent with their holy calling (4:1).

In verse 4, Paul penned his second terrible trio. This trio deals with sinful speech regarding sex: (1) obscene language; (2) foolish talk; and (3) coarse jesting. **Foolish talk** refers to futile talk that detracts from faith and edifying discussion.

Giving of thanks is a strong contrast to forms of immorality, greed, and sinful language. This activity and lifestyle glorify God.

Thought for the Day: Are greed and impure thoughts present in your thought life? Are your language and speech always Christ like?

TWO WARNINGS FROM PAUL!

For this you know with certainty, that no immoral or impure person or covetous man, who is an idolater, has an inheritance in the kingdom of Christ and God. 6 Let no one deceive you with empty words, for because of these things the wrath of God comes upon the sons of disobedience. 7 Therefore do not be partakers with them.—**Eph. 5:5–7**

Here Paul gave one of his most severe warnings. The **immoral** Christian breaks the *seventh* commandment (committing adultery) as well as the *tenth* commandment (do not covet your neighbor's wife). Paul described an immoral, impure or covetous person as an **idolater.** Sexual lust is an idolatrous obsession because it places self-gratification or another person at the center of one's life. When a believer puts any person or thing before God, the believer breaks the *first* commandment (no other gods before Me). If the believer has an idol (such as sex) in his/her life, commandment *two* (You shall not make for yourselves an idol,...) is also broken.

In his second warning (v. 6), Paul urged his readers not to be misled by anyone who encourages sexual permissiveness. Arguments of this kind consist of **empty words** because they do not consider God's judgment on sin. Christians are not to be indifferent to the sin of sexual permissiveness.

Wrath is God's personal reaction against sin. God will inflict vengeance upon those who do not obey His Word. Because the consequences of an immoral lifestyle are so serious (will not inherit kingdom of God), Paul urged the Ephesian believers not to participate with disobedient Gentiles in their sinful behavior (v. 7).

Thought for the Day: Can your lifestyle be characterized as: immoral, impure, or covetous? If so, repent so you may inherit the kingdom of God.

YOU ARE LIGHT IN THE LORD

For you were formerly darkness, but now you are Light in the Lord; walk as children of the Light **9** *(for the fruit of the Light consists in all goodness and righteousness and truth),* **10** *trying to learn what is pleasing to the Lord.*—**Eph. 5:8–10**

In verses 8-14 Paul continued a contrast between **light** and **darkness**. Once Paul's Ephesian readers were unbelievers and belonged to Satan's dominion of darkness. Darkness is used metaphorically as a symbol of ignorance, error, evil, and blindness. Now, through their relationship with Christ, they are members of the realm of "light" (v. 8).

In Ephesians, "light" stands for *truth, knowledge* (1:18), and here, *holiness* (v. 8) which all come from God. Their radical transformation, which occurred at conversion, had taken place **in the Lord**.

Paul explained what it means to live as **children of light** by listing three Christian graces that he described as the **fruit of the Light**. He used "fruit" in a *figurative* way to denote the result of becoming children of light or children of God. Paul viewed light as a divine power. **Goodness**, **righteousness**, and **truth** are supernatural characteristics that result from God's activity in believers. Paul balanced divine activity and human response or responsibility. Fruit of the light is similar in meaning to "fruit of the Spirit" (Gal. 5:22).

In verse 10, Paul informed his readers of the manner in which he expected them to live—they were directed to discern or **to learn what is pleasing to the Lord**. *Discern* means to examine and evaluate issues to determine the correct course of action. In a practical way, the Word (Bible) and the Holy Spirit help Christians learn what actions, activities and attitudes please the Lord.

Thought for the Day: Is your life pleasing to the Lord?

DO NOT PARTICIPATE IN UNFRUITFUL DEEDS OF DARKNESS

*Do not participate in the unfruitful deeds of darkness, but instead even expose them; **12** for it is disgraceful even to speak of the things which are done by them in secret.*—**Eph. 5:11–12**

Yesterday we discussed what is pleasing to the Lord (v. 10).

In verse 11, with "unfruitful deeds of darkness," Paul referred the readers back to verse 7. There he told readers not to be partakers with the pagan, immoral Gentiles, whom he called "sons of disobedience" in verse 6b. The **unfruitful deeds of darkness** are a stark contrast to "fruit of the light" (v. 9) that produces goodness and righteousness and truth. The first command in verse 11 is negative and is similar to Paul's command in verse 7—"Therefore do not be partakers with them."

Paul followed his negative command with a positive exhortation. The Ephesian believers are to bring to light or **expose** the unfruitful deeds of darkness performed by the unbelievers around them. They will expose the sin of unbelievers by living godly lifestyles (goodness, righteousness, and truth) and showing the unbelievers' "unfruitful deeds" to be evil.

In verse 12, Paul gave another reason for his two exhortations in verse 11. The sins of the unbelievers are so horrible, Paul exclaimed that it was **disgraceful even** to mention them specifically.

Paul's contrast of darkness versus light is enhanced by the idea of *secrecy*. "Unfruitful deeds of darkness" (v. 11) is general and probably refers to sins committed both openly and secretly. Paul desired the "light" of the gospel to shine through the lives of his readers to **expose** the deeds of unbelievers for what they are—*unfruitful deeds of darkness*.

Thought for the Day: Is your day-to-day lifestyle exposing the evil deeds of unbelievers around you for what they are—sinful?

79

EXPOSED BY THE LIGHT

But all things become visible when they are exposed by
the light, for everything that becomes visible is light. **14**
For this reason it says, "Awake, sleeper, and arise from
the dead, and Christ will shine on you."—**Eph. 5:13–14**

All things refers to all sin that is done in secret (v. 12b). Paul
was probably thinking primarily of hidden sexual sins. In
verse 11, Paul instructed his readers to expose the unfruitful works
of darkness.

There is a two-fold value of a Christian exposure of evil. First,
when any sin is exposed by the light it becomes visible. Second,
anything that **becomes visible is light**. Paul seems to be teaching
that light transforms what it illumines into light. Therefore, as one
Christian's light exposes the sin of an unbeliever, that unbeliever
may turn to Christ and become "light." The light given off by
believers may bring unbelievers to the conviction of their sin and to
faith in Christ. Light not only has the power to convict, it has the
ability to transform.

In verse 14, Paul addressed the person as a **sleeper** (a less
offensive term for death or a dead person). In this context, sleep,
death, and darkness are striking images that described the condition
of the individual apart from Christ. The unbeliever is in a state of
spiritual death (sleep).

Paul's call to **awake and arise from the dead** refers to
repentance that occurs at conversion. This involves being brought
out of darkness into the light of Christ. **Shine** is an intense verb that
conveys the idea of dominating, transforming light in the midst of
darkness. Christ is that transforming "light." He, in line with OT
Scripture and imagery, has *shined* upon His people and saved them.

Thought for the Day: Is the "light" from your life convicting
any of your unbelieving friends and co-workers?

BE CAREFUL HOW YOU WALK

Therefore be careful how you walk, not as unwise men but as
wise, **16** making the most of your time, because the days are
evil.—**Eph. 5:15–16**

Verses 15–21 may be considered a *summary* of Paul's
exhortations in chapters 4 through 6. Paul used the word
walk in four preceding paragraphs (4:1–16; 4:17–24; 4:25–5:2 and
5:3–14).

Paul applied the metaphor of **walking** to refer to general
Christian living. In 4:1 his call to walk worthy of our calling is a
general command. In 5:15–21 he gave his readers specifics regarding
their "walk" or Christian lifestyle.

If the readers are careful how they walk, they will live as **wise**
men and women. In the previous paragraph (5:3–14), Paul
contrasted light and darkness. In this paragraph, Paul drew a
contrast between wise and **unwise.** A wise person's wisdom is
divine in nature and origin. The unwise walk as those who have no
insight into God's revealed will.

In verse 16, Paul explained in more concrete terms what he
meant by "be careful how you walk." A wise person realizes time is
passing quickly. Therefore, wise Christians will "make the most" or
make good use of the time God gives them.

Now, Paul gave the reason for his earlier command. He referred
to the present age ("the days") as evil. Probably moral, more than
physical evil, was in Paul's mind. **The days are evil** because they are
controlled by the god of this age, Satan (Eph. 2:2 and 2 Cor. 4:4).

Thought for the Day: Are you snatching up every
opportunity to live a life before unbelievers which glorifies
God?

81

UNDERSTAND THE LORD'S WILL

So then do not be foolish, but understand what the will of the
Lord is. **18** And do not get drunk with wine, for that is dissipation,
but be filled with the Spirit.—**Eph. 5:17–18**

Paul informed his readers, using the contrast **not drunk with wine, but filled with the Spirit**, how to specifically apply his command "be careful how you walk" (v. 15a).

The adjective **foolish** in the OT describes the fool, one who is careless, lacks understanding and despises wisdom (Prov. 1:18, 23; 14:26; 17:18). In contrast, the *wise* believer perceives or comprehends the will of the Lord. Wise Christians realize that wisdom is found in God's will and it comes from God.

In verse 18, Paul noted that being drunk with wine leads to **dissipation**, while being "filled with the Spirit" leads to joy in fellowship and obedience to God. To get drunk is "foolish" or unwise conduct. *Dissipation* (sexual excesses and debauchery) and unrestrained living may eventually lead to ruin. An inebriated person is under the influence of alcohol, while a Spirit-filled Christian is under the influence and power of the Holy Spirit.

To be **filled with the Spirit** means to be transformed by the Spirit into the likeness of God and Christ. "To be filled" is a present passive verb in the Greek. The present tense indicates a repeated action of filling by the Holy Spirit. The passive mood shows God accomplishes this total infilling as believers allow the Holy Spirit to work in their individual lives. The interplay between the divine sovereignty and *human responsibility* is evident here.

Thought for the Day: Are you regularly being "filled with the Spirit" and allowing the Spirit to change you more and more into the image of Christ?

CHARACTERISTICS OF
BEING FILLED WITH THE SPIRIT

Speaking to one another in psalms and hymns and spiritual
songs, singing and making melody with your heart to the Lord; **20**
always giving thanks for all things in the name of our Lord Jesus
Christ to God, even the Father; **21** and be subject to one another
in the fear of Christ.—**Eph. 5:19–21**

In verse 18, Paul exhorted his readers to 'be filled with the
Spirit.' In the verses today, we see five participles that modify
his command.

Verse 19 is composed of two parallel halves that should be
interpreted together. It describes the **singing** of psalms, hymns, and
spiritual songs by believers who are Spirit-filled. However, verses
19a and 19b come at the singing from two different, but related
standpoints. First, believers are **speaking** to one another in psalms,
hymns and spiritual songs. Evidently the believers are reminding
each other of what God has accomplished in Christ. It appears the
purpose of their singing is to instruct and edify each other. Second, in
verse 19b, the singing and **making melody** are directed to the Lord.
This part of the verse seems to have a corporate dimension (church)
and a *vertical* focus—to Jesus.

Spirit-filled Christians also will regularly be **giving** thanks for all
things to God the Father in the Son's name. It follows that believers
are to give God thanks during times of trial and suffering, too.

To **be subject to** (v. 21) means literally to "arrange under."
Therefore, Spirit-filled believers are to be mutually submissive to
one another. "In the fear of Christ" provided the *motivation* for
believers to be mutually submissive to one another.

Thought for the Day: Does melody break forth in your heart
as you think about all the Lord has done for you?

WIVES SUBMIT TO YOUR HUSBANDS

Wives, be subject to your own husbands, as to the Lord.—**Eph. 5:22**

The section from 5:22 to 6:9 is commonly termed the *household code*. The first set (vv. 22–33) of three sets of exhortations is addressed to wives and husbands (5:22–33).

In NT times, most marriages took place without power being transferred from the wife's father to her husband. Consequently, wives exercised a greater degree of independence from their husbands than in early Greek and Roman households. The hierarchical pattern of the household code reflected a patriarchal model that is also a *creational* model.

Hellenistic Jews (Jews who spoke Greek and adopted Greek ideas) and Judaism viewed women as inferior to men. However, Paul viewed **wives** as equal to husbands qualitatively and subordinate to men with regard to the lines of authority. Verse 22 does not contain a verb. However, the theme of submission carries over in this context from verse 21. Therefore, Paul's imperative **be subject** is understood.

At the center of submission is the idea of order. God established leadership and authority roles within the family. Consequently, submission to authority is the recognition of His divine ordering.

This phrase **as to the Lord** supplies the *motivation* for the wife to be subject to her husband. By being submissive to her husband, she is also submitting to the Lord. Being submissive to her husband is not a separate action from being submissive to Christ. Instead, it is one key way she serves and obeys the Lord.

Thought for the Day: One of the most evident characteristics that Christians are being "filled with the Spirit" is their submissiveness to one another and to Christ.

THE HUSBAND IS THE HEAD OF THE WIFE

For the husband is the head of the wife, as Christ also is the head of the church, He Himself being the Savior of the body.—**Eph. 5:23**

In the early Roman Empire of Paul's day, there was a trend toward the wife's father, rather than her husband, having authority over the wife as long as the father lived. In some cases, the wife was independent from and not legally subject to her husband.

In 1:22 and 4:15, Paul used the term **head**. However, here, for the first time, the husband's headship is stated as a fact. Also, his headship is the basis of his wife's submission. Paul's statement confronted the family structure of that day by telling readers the husband, not the wife's father, has authority over the wife. The husband's headship and the wife's submission are practical realities ordained by God to promote harmony within the family.

Paul made the headship of the husband parallel to Christ's headship or rule over the church. With this clause, Paul presented the reason for the wife's submission to her husband. In this passage, it is important to understand the headship of Christ over His church. As its head, Christ has "authority over" the church.

Paul used **Savior of the body** to remind his readers that Christ delivered the body from eternal doom. With this analogy, Paul was not indicating the husband spiritually "saves" his wife. Instead, Paul was referring to the fact the husband should protect his wife in times of physical or spiritual danger. The husband's positon of authority over his wife must include a protective quality, which is exemplified in Christ—the Savior of the body.

Thought for the Day: Thank God today that in His wisdom and love He ordained authority within the family.

THE CHURCH AND WIVES IN SUBMISSION

But as the church is subject to Christ, so also the wives ought to be to their husbands in everything.—**Eph. 5:24**

The clause as the **church is subject to Christ** stands in comparison with "so also the wives ought to be to their husbands." Paul made a direct comparison between the church being submissive to Christ and the wife being submissive to her husband. As the church benefits from the headship of Christ, the wife's submission to her husband should enhance her well-being. The church's submission to Christ is the model of the wife's submission to her husband.

The church receives many, many *blessings* from Christ, including: (1) Christ's gifts of grace, 4:7; (2) ministers to whom God gives gifts, 4:11; and (3) all that is necessary for spiritual growth, 4:15, 16.

The church's submission to Christ means looking to its head for His beneficial rule, living by His norms (Matt. 5:3–7:27), experiencing His presence and love, and responding to Him with gratitude. Paul urged the wife to develop these attitudes and consistent actions as she submits to her husband.

The phrase **in everything** indicates the wife is to be subordinate to her husband in every area of life. Therefore, no part of her life should be outside the sphere of her subordination to her husband. "In everything" must be read within the context of this chapter and other Scriptures. So, wives are not required by God to be subordinate to husbands in matters that are sinful or contrary to God's commands. Yet, there is no suggestion that wives are to be submissive to their husbands only if their husbands are loving.

Thought for the Day: The wife's submission to her husband will lead to God's blessing—for others, including her husband, and herself.

HUSBANDS, LOVE YOUR WIVES—PART I

*Husbands, love your wives, just as Christ also loved the church and gave Himself up for her.—**Eph. 5:25***

In verses 22–24, Paul dealt with the extent of the wife's submission to her husband. Then, in verses 25–32, he addressed the measure of the husband's love for his wife.

The wife's submission to her husband has its counterpart in the husband's duty and responsibility to **love** his wife. Paul did *not* exhort husbands to rule over their wives. Instead, he commanded husbands to love (also vv. 28 and 33) their wives. The Greek word for love (*agape*) here means *God's love*. Therefore, Paul exhorted husbands to show unceasing care and loving service for the well-being of their wives in all areas—physical, mental, and spiritual. In addition, the husband's love for his wife is to be an ongoing process. Husbands must love their wives *unconditionally*, even when they may seem undeserving and unloving.

The *pattern* for the husband's love for his wife is Christ's love for His church. This is a *radical* love—that led Jesus to die on a cruel cross for sinful humanity. In addition, this is *self-sacrificing* love. This verse can be interpreted as teaching that husbands are to sacrifice their interests for the welfare of their wives. Taken literally, the second part of verse 25 teaches that husbands should be willing to make even the ultimate sacrifice (life itself) for their wives! Husbands are to imitate the sacrificial love of Christ in their marriages.

If husbands obey Paul's command, they will not behave in an overbearing way toward their wives. Instead, all areas of married life will be characterized by self-sacrificing love.

Thought for the Day: As a husband, are you loving your wife sacrificially?

CHRIST WILL SANCTIFY HIS BRIDE

*So that He might sanctify her, having cleansed her by the washing of water with the word, **27** that He might present to Himself the church in all her glory, having no spot or wrinkle or any such thing; but that she would be holy and blameless.—**Eph. 5:26–27***

Today we will look at three **purposes** of Christ's sacrificial love for the church: (1) that He might sanctify her, v. 26; (2) that He might present to Himself the church, v. 27a; and (3) that she might be holy and without blame, v. 27c.

That he might **sanctify her** refers to the fact the church was set aside to God for His service. "Having cleansed her" refers to Christ morally cleansing the church. This cleansing probably happens simultaneously with His sanctifying her (v. 26) and making her **holy** (v. 27). Christ accomplished the cleansing by the **washing of water with the word**. By washing, Paul reminded his readers of the church's spiritual cleansing. "With the word" refers to the word of the gospel.

Christ presents to Himself the church as His bride. It is likely Paul believed this will occur at the second coming of Christ. Then the glorified church will be with Christ forever and will be glorious. **Having no spot or wrinkle** shows the unsurpassed beauty of Christ's bride when He presents her to Himself. At His second coming, His bride will have no physical imperfection, a metaphorical way to address the church's *moral perfection.*

That she **would be holy and blameless** tells of a beauty that is both moral and spiritual. Holiness and its accompanying blamelessness will characterize Christ's bride at His second coming.

Thought for the Day: Thank God that at the second coming of Christ you will have no "spot or wrinkle." Instead, you will stand morally and spiritually perfect before Christ.

HUSBANDS, LOVE YOUR WIVES—PART II

So husbands ought also to love their own wives as their own
bodies. He who loves his own wife loves himself; **29** for no one
ever hated his own flesh, but nourishes and cherishes it, just as
Christ also does the church.—**Eph. 5:28–29**

The closing application is taken from Christ's love for His church as husbands are again urged to love their wives.

Paul again focused on the extent of *love* a **husband** should have for his wife. In marriage, husband and wife are one flesh (Gen. 2:24). In Ephesians, "flesh" and "body" are synonymous. The husband has a responsibility to love himself. Then he is more likely to love his wife.

Paul's focus here was on the extent of love a husband should have for his wife. No one ever **hated his own flesh** (v. 29) is probably a general or proverbial truth from Paul's day. Paul elaborated on the idea of taking care of one's body by using the phrase **he nourishes and cherishes it**. These terms are metaphorical and appear to be taken from the nursery. They are the opposite of hating one's body (v. 29). "To nourish" means "to bring up from childhood." Here the word has the connotation of a parent who nurtures a child. To *cherish* meant literally, "to heat." Here, it means "to take tender care of" much in the way a man cares for his own body. These two terms express appropriate behavior on the part of the husband toward the wife, because they have become "one flesh" (5:31).

As it is natural for a man not to hate his own flesh but to nourish it, so it is also natural for Christ to nurture and take care of His body, the church.

Thought for the Day: Praise God today that His Son *nourishes* (brings you up from childhood) and *cherishes* (takes tender care of) you.

WE ARE MEMBERS OF HIS BODY

Because we are members of His body.—**Eph. 5:30**

Next Paul introduced the reason Christ nurtures and takes care of His church—we are members of His body.

The Greek word **member** has a literal reference to limbs or members of a *living* body, whether human or animal. This Greek noun *member* is never used of a member of an inanimate organization. Instead, it is always used of a member of a **living** organism, such as a hand, a leg, or an arm.

We see Paul used *member* metaphorically. Paul employed this term to teach that believers are members of Christ (1 Cor. 6:15). In the literal, physical realm, different members have different functions. So, in the spiritual analogy, members are different but experience unity and harmony as they help the body function effectively. The unity of members is not due to external organization but to the common, vital union they all share in Christ.

In addition, Paul used the term **body** to express the *oneness* of the church with Her Lord. The primary emphasis of the body metaphor was to picture the unity of believers with Christ.

The widespread tradition of formal church membership is **not** related to the metaphorical and biblical concept of "members of His body." Instead, Paul used the noun *member* to demonstrate the close-knit relationship of individual members of the body with Christ, its head.

Note that Paul said, "we are members of His body," instead of "you are members of His body." Paul and his readers were so intimately and closely joined to Christ that they were becoming part of Christ. He and his readers had become incorporated into Christ and were members of the body that He nourishes and cherishes (5:29).

Thought for the Day: Praise God that as a "member" of the living body of Christ, the church, you are nourished and cherished by Christ.

HUSBANDS, LOVE YOUR WIVES—PART III

FOR THIS REASON A MAN SHALL LEAVE HIS FATHER AND
MOTHER AND SHALL BE JOINED TO HIS WIFE, AND THE TWO
SHALL BECOME ONE FLESH. **32** This mystery is great; but I am
speaking with reference to Christ and the church. **33**
Nevertheless, each individual among you also is to love his own
wife even as himself, and the wife must see to it that she
respects her husband.—**Eph. 5:31–33**

Verse 31 is a quotation of Genesis 2:24. This reinforced Paul's argument that the husband is compelled to love his wife because they are **one flesh** and no one hates his own flesh or body. The Hebrew verb **be joined** means "to glue" or "to cement" as when two metals are welded together. Consequently, the husband and wife are to be *glued* to each other.

Mystery refers to the relationship between Christ and the church, of which marriage is *a type*. The parallels between the two concepts of marriage making husband and wife one body and the close union between Christ and the church are key to Paul's argument in chapter 5.

In verse 33 Paul returned to the main subject—authority within marriage. He completed his discussion with two summarizing exhortations that restate the *duties* and *responsibilities* of husbands and wives. The husband is to **love** his wife as himself because she is united with him. The wife is to **respect** her husband. The Greek word carries the idea of *fear* rather than respect. Fear can be defined as *reverence* for her husband's God-given position as head of the home. In verse 21, the "fear of Christ" provided the *motivation* for believers to be mutually submissive to one another.

Thought for the Day: Praise God today for the great "mystery"—the close relationship between members of the body and Christ.

CHILDREN, OBEY YOUR PARENTS

Children, obey your parents in the Lord, for this is
right. **2** HONOR YOUR FATHER AND MOTHER (which is
the first commandment with a promise), **3** SO THAT IT
MAY BE WELL WITH YOU, AND THAT YOU MAY LIVE
LONG ON THE EARTH.—**Eph. 6:1–3**

After giving wives and husbands several exhortations (vv. 22–33), Paul dealt with duties of children and their parents (6:1–4).

The term **children** in the Greek language denotes primarily *relationship* rather than age. In some cases, young adult sons and daughters could be included in this verse because they were expected to honor their parents, especially their fathers. Fathers could maintain authority in the family until death.

The verb **obey** is a present imperative, stressing the obedience of children is an ongoing action and denoting the absolute obedience to parents. **In the Lord** gives a *motivation* for their obedience and indicates obedience to parents is part of their Christian discipleship. Also, this phrase emphasized that a child's ultimate obedience is to the Lord. **For this is right** gives another *motivation* for obedience.

In verse 2 Paul quoted the first part of the fifth commandment to support his instruction. The mother was equal to the father and had equal claim on the obedience of the children (Ex. 20:12).

Verse 3 comprises Paul's paraphrase of the promise associated with the fifth commandment. During OT times, children who continued to be disobedient to parents could be stoned, according to provisions of the Mosaic law. By contrast, if children obeyed their parents, their lives were *not* shortened through stoning. Paul was probably alluding to these OT laws.

Thought for the Day: Thank God for your parents and praise Him additionally if they are Christians.

FATHERS, DO NOT PROVOKE YOUR CHILDREN

Fathers, do not provoke your children to anger, but bring them up in the discipline and instruction of the Lord.—**Eph. 6:4**

You will note Paul did not include mothers here. In hierarchical structures of Paul's day, the husband was responsible for the entire family. Paul presented **the fathers** with a new perspective on the treatment of their children. Under Roman law, fathers had absolute control. Paul did not say anything of their right to absolute control over their children. Instead, Paul gave a negative and then a positive exhortation to fathers.

Paul exhorted fathers not to **provoke** their children to anger. By this command, Paul was urging fathers to avoid attitudes, words, and actions that would cause their children to become angry. His command would rule out such things as excessive discipline, unreasonably harsh demands, condemnation, humiliation, constant nagging, and manipulation.

Then Paul complemented his negative instruction with a positive one. The Greek verb **bring them up** is used of raising children from childhood to maturity.

The two nouns "discipline" and "instruction" have slightly different meanings. Discipline can refer to education in a comprehensive sense. *Instruction* involves the more specific aspect of this training that takes place with verbal warning or correction.

Of the Lord describes the type of discipline and instruction that fathers were commanded to give. The discipline and instruction had Christ as its reference point. Consequently, Christian fathers were to be different from the unbelieving fathers of their society.

Thought for the Day: Praise God that Christian fathers are to care for their families as God cares for His family!

93

INSTRUCTIONS TO SLAVES

Slaves, be obedient to those who are your masters according to the flesh, with fear and trembling, in the sincerity of your heart, as to Christ; **6** not by way of eye service, as men-pleasers, but as slaves of Christ, doing the will of God from the heart. **7** With good will render service, as to the Lord, and not to men, **8** knowing that whatever good thing each one does, this he will receive back from the Lord, whether slave or free.—**Eph. 6:5-8**

In these verses, Paul addressed believing slaves who were probably part of the church at Ephesus. The opening and key admonition is **be obedient to** earthly **masters**. "Fear and trembling" denote the state of mind. Masters controlled their slaves primarily by fear. Fear also can be interpreted here as *respect*. Service to masters was to be with pure motives and *sincerity* of heart. **As to Christ** reminded slaves that they were in the presence of God the Father and Christ as they worked.

Paul commanded slaves to obey their masters with integrity—not to be obedient by way of **eye service**. Eye service probably is the kind of performance done merely to impress the master and leave undone anything he would not notice. **From the heart** means slaves are to obey their masters from their innermost beings.

Paul reminded them they are to labor heartily each day as if they are also working directly for the Lord and not merely for their human lords. Their *motivation* for this kind of labor and attitude is the fact they are serving **the Lord** and not simply humans. In verse 8, Paul reminded them that they will be rewarded by their heavenly Lord at the final judgment for the good they did on earth.

Thought for the Day: Remember that you will one day stand before Christ at the judgment and receive a reward for the good works you have done.

INSTRUCTIONS TO MASTERS

And masters, do the same things to them, and give up threatening, knowing that both their Master and yours is in heaven, and there is no partiality with Him.—**Eph. 6:9**

Then Paul turned to the masters and exhorted them regarding their responsibilities to their slaves. You will note that Paul first addressed the slaves (vv. 5–8).

Here Paul made a connection between his previous exhortation to slaves ("do the same things to them") and his current exhortation to **masters**. With this approach, he underscored the reciprocal relationships that should exist between slaves and masters.

Considering the state of the first century Greco-Roman world, Paul made a shocking exhortation. In this time and culture, many masters considered their slaves *enemies*. Unfortunately, many masters were abusive. Also, many masters **threatened** beatings, sexual harassment, or selling male slaves away from their households. In contrast, Paul exhorted the masters, like their slaves, to: be sincere (v. 5), do the will of God from the heart (v. 6) and with good will render service as to the Lord (v. 7). Consequently, Paul's commands in verse 9 struck a blow at considering their slaves as *enemies*.

knowing that both their Master and yours is in heaven

Paul appeals to masters in two main ways. First, the slaves' Master and their Master is the Lord of heaven and both parties are accountable to Him. Masters are reminded that they also are slaves, fellow slaves of the same Lord as their servants. This truth should humble masters. Second, Paul appealed to masters by reminding them that their higher social status gave them no advantage—the Lord is absolutely *impartial*.

Thought for the Day: Whether a supervisor or a subordinate, you are ultimately accountable to the Lord.

BE STRONG IN THE LORD!

Finally, be strong in the Lord and in the strength of His might.—**Eph. 6:10**

Paul's command to **be strong** refers to explosive strength, ability, or power. This Greek verb (*endunamos*) conveys the idea of being infused with a large dose of dynamic inner strength and ability. As mere weak mortals, we are in great need of daily doses of divine help. The command to "be strong" is in the present passive imperative. This tense indicates the believer is to be continually allowing the Holy Spirit to strengthen him or her with power. The passive mood of "be strong" indicates each believer receives from God the action of being strengthened. Therefore, Paul commanded them to open their hearts continually and receive new infusions of God's power.

This special power is found only **in the Lord**. Because we are in the Lord, we are never far from a fresh surge of divine power. This flow of divine power is a work of grace and not of human effort. However, if believers temporarily cease to walk in fellowship with God, they are choosing to stop the flow of this divine power into their lives. **In the strength** describes power that is demonstrative and tangible (1:19–20). The Greek word for "strength" (*kratos*) here is the same word used for the power God exercised when He resurrected Jesus. Without this power operating in our lives, we cannot successfully engage in battle with the enemy.

Of His might involves another Greek word (*ischuos*) for power. This noun conveys the picture of a body builder. Paul applied the image of a strong, muscular man to God. The reason the *strength* (*kratos*) of God is so powerful and demonstrative (resulted in the resurrection) is that God's "might" (*ischuos*) is backing it up.

Thought for the Day: Ask God to infuse your spirit with a dose of His dynamic strength—strength with which He resurrected Jesus!

PUT ON THE FULL ARMOR OF GOD

*Put on the full armor of God, so that you will be able to stand
firm against the schemes of the devil.*—**Eph. 6:11**

In this passage on spiritual warfare (vv. 10–18), armor is almost
entirely concerned with our spiritual protection—the *defensive*
struggle with the devil, principalities, and powers.

In today's verse Paul used a metaphor—**put on** (see 4:24). To *put
on* denotes the act of donning a new set of clothes. Here Paul used
this clothing metaphor in connection with putting on spiritual armor.
The verb "put on" is in the middle voice. This indicates Christians are
responsible for putting on the armor. It is the Lord's armor, but we
must take it up and put it on!

Paul no doubt had the Roman foot soldier in mind as he penned
this verse. The Roman soldier possessed six pieces of armor. Paul
commanded his readers to put on the **full armor**. In other words,
Paul instructed his readers to put on all six pieces. **Of God** reminded
them that every piece of their supernatural set of weaponry came
directly from God. In addition, none of them (or us!) could use this
armor if we had not first been given the spiritual strength required
to use it (v. 10).

That you might be able could be translated "that you may have
explosive, dynamic power to." **To stand** is used in a military sense. It
means to maintain a critical, strategic military position over a
battlefield. This implies the Christian has a responsibility to stand
guard over the battlefield of his or her life. By using *to stand firm
against*, Paul was portraying a bold soldier glaring fearlessly into the
eyes of his enemy.

Schemes in the Greek language literally means "with a road." This
indicates the enemy travels on one road or avenue. Satan's road is

headed toward the mind of the believer. Therefore, Satan seeks to penetrate a believer's mind so he can flood it with deception and falsehood.

Thought for the Day: Think of yourself as a soldier enlisted in the army of the living God "standing firm against" Satan and his demon hosts.

Notes:

_____

_____

_____

_____

_____

_____

SPIRITUAL WARFARE

For our struggle is not against flesh and blood, but against the rulers, against the powers, against the world forces of this darkness, against the spiritual forces of wickedness in the heavenly places.—**Eph. 6:12**

Paul realized the present evil age is in the grip of evil supernatural powers. **Angels** are beings created for the purpose of serving God. They are spectators of the human scene (1 Cor. 4:9; 11:10). Unfortunately, part of the angelic world (evil spirits) has rebelled against God and has become hostile to God and His purposes. Angels often operate on a more localized or individual level than the **evil spirits**.

Demons are fallen angels, also labeled "evil spirits" (Matt. 8:16; 17:18; Luke 10:17). Their nature is spiritual because, like Satan, they lack physical bodies (Eph. 2:2, 6:12). As spiritual beings, they operate above the laws of the natural realm. They possess super-human intellect and because of their evil and depraved moral nature they derange their victims mentally, morally, physically, and spiritually. They can inflict *blindness* (Matt. 12:22), *insanity* (Luke 8:26–36), and *dumbness* (Matt. 9:32–33). Under the leadership of Satan, demons seek to oppose God's purposes and hinder man's welfare.

Satan, sometimes called the devil, is an evil spirit and the archenemy of God. He is the "prince of the power of the air" (Eph. 2:2) and the god of this age (2 Cor. 4:4). Paul used other language to designate ranks of evil angelic spirits—**rulers**, **powers**, **world forces of this darkness**, and "spiritual forces of wickedness." God's purpose is to display to these principalities and powers in the heavenly places the manifold wisdom of God through the church (Eph. 3:10).

Thought for the Day: Praise God that these evil powers have been brought into subordination by Christ's death and resurrection!

TAKE UP THE FULL ARMOR OF GOD

Therefore, take up the full armor of God, so that you will be able to resist in the evil day, and having done everything, to stand firm.—**Eph. 6:13**

Here Paul restated his exhortation of verse 11—to put on the *full armor of God.* The verb **take up** refers to putting on weapons. The command is in the active voice which indicates that believers are responsible for putting on the full armor. **So that you will be able to resist** gives the *purpose* of putting on the complete armor of God. *To resist* or withstand (KJV) means "to set against." It is in the past tense and active voice. The active voice indicates it is an action done by the individual believer. This verb signifies a *defensive* stance.

In the evil day probably refers basically to one's Christian life on earth. Also, Paul may have been including more critical times in the lives of believers when demonic hostility is especially intense. Paul was reminding his readers they must not be lulled into a false sense of security during more peaceful times—times of reprieve from intense Satanic powers. Therefore, His readers must be prepared always by having on "the full armor of God."

Having done everything probably refers to having strapped on all the armor. **To stand firm** gives the idea of steadfastness as one stands before his or her spiritual enemies. This is a synonym for "to resist," used earlier in this verse. When the believer has "done everything," he or she is prepared to stand firm against Satan and his evil forces. The devil and his angels are strong, but not omnipotent (all-powerful), as is God.

Thought for the Day: This verse is not about victory or defeat, but holding fast to territory already won by Christ. In your spiritual warfare, are you "holding fast" to territory already conquered by Christ?

STAND, AND PUT ON THE LOIN BELT OF TRUTH

Stand firm therefore, HAVING GIRDED YOUR LOINS WITH
TRUTH.—**Eph. 6:14a**

The command **stand firm** appears for the third time (also, vv. 11, 13). The exhortation's repetition heightens its sense of urgency. *Stand firm* is the main admonition of this passage. Rich in military metaphor, it refers to the stance of a soldier in combat who resolutely opposes the enemy. **Having girded your loins** is in the middle voice. This indicates Christians are responsible to gird themselves.

Of all the pieces of armor, the *loin belt* or girdle was the most vital. It was the first item to be put on and held many pieces of his armor. The shield was attached to it and his sword hung from it. It also kept the breastplate from flapping in the wind.

The loin belt, made of loose or sewn thongs of leather, hung under the armor and protected the soldier's thighs. In addition, the soldier fastened articles of clothing on the loin belt or tucked the long skirts of his robe under it. This freed the soldier for a greater range and ease of movement during battle.

Christian soldiers are to gird their waists with God's **truth** that is found in the Bible. The written word of God is the most important piece of weaponry the Christian soldier possesses. To be clothed in your spiritual armor, you must begin by taking up the Word of God. Then allow it to lead, guide, and equip you. If you do not have the loin belt of truth girding the loins and your *life*, your *heart*, and your *mind*, you will not be able to walk with the other pieces of armor God makes available to you.

Thought for the Day: Do you read the Bible daily to allow God to gird up the loins of your heart and mind with His truth?

101

STAND, AND PUT ON
THE BREASTPLATE OF RIGHTEOUSNESS

And having put on the breastplate of righteousness.—**Eph. 6:14b**

The second piece of spiritual armor is the **breastplate of righteousness**. Righteousness is judged by the standard of God's holy law, derived from His holy character. Because of the results of Adam's sin (Rom. 5:12–21), mankind is corrupt, lacks righteousness (Rom. 3:23), and cannot make himself righteous. However, through the atoning work of Christ, man can be given righteousness. God views Christians as "righteous" (justified).

The breastplate was the shiniest, most beautiful piece of armor. Also, it was the heaviest piece weighing forty or more pounds, usually made of brass. It extended from the top of the soldier's neck to just above his knees thus protecting the chest and abdomen. It is vitally important to protect the heart where feelings, affections, and desires are controlled because Satan and his hosts attempt to create inordinate desires. As the breastplate protected his chest, sanctified living guards the believer's heart against the assaults of the devil.

There are two kinds of righteousness in the life of a Christian— **imputed** and **imparted**. When a person accepts Christ as Savior, he/she is *justified* by faith. This makes the person forensically right with the demands of the law because of the *atonement* of Christ (2 Cor. 5:21). In justification, righteousness is *imputed* to the believer. In the process of *progressive sanctification*, a person is progressively made more righteous in character and conduct (1 John 1:7–9; 2 Cor. 3:18; 2 Peter 3:18) and God's righteousness is *imparted* to the Christian. As Christians study the Bible and understand both God's imputed and His imparted righteousness, their new sense of personal righteousness will impart confidence to their spiritual lives.

Thought for the Day: To be emotionally, spiritually, and mentally prepared for battle, believers must know they are *righteous* in Christ. Do you?

STAND, HAVING SHOD YOUR FEET WITH THE PREPARATION OF THE GOSPEL OF PEACE

And having shod YOUR FEET WITH THE PREPARATION OF THE
GOSPEL OF PEACE.—**Eph. 6:15**

The third piece of spiritual armor Paul specified was to have one's **feet shod** with the preparation of the gospel of peace. The Roman soldier's feet were shod with heavy sandals. Their soles were made of several layers of leather reaching a total thickness of three-fourths of an inch. These thick soles were studded with hollow-headed hobnails. The sandals were tied on by a series of leather thongs extending half way up the shin. These heavy sandals gave them a firm footing on the battlefield.

Preparation can have meanings of both readiness and preparation. Preparation in the Greek language can also convey the idea of a firm footing or foundation.

Some facts can be noted regarding the gospel and the **gospel of peace**. First, Satan fears and hates the gospel because it is God's power to rescue people from his tyranny. Second, as believers trust the Christ of the gospel daily for salvation, He continues to give them spiritual victory and power. Third, the gospel is the firm footing of the Christian soldier. Fourth, when people accept the gospel they have peace with God. *Peace* is practically synonymous with *salvation* (Rom. 2:10). The "peace of God" is a power that *protects* man in his inner being (Phil. 4:7) and *guards* the hearts and minds of believers. Because they are firmly grounded in the "gospel of peace," they are prepared to stand firm against the onslaughts of evil forces.

Thought for the Day: Can you victoriously say with Paul, "I am not ashamed of the gospel, for it is the power of God for salvation to everyone who believes, to the Jew first and also to the Greek" (Rom. 1:16)

TAKE UP THE SHIELD OF FAITH—PART I

In addition to all, taking up the shield of faith with which you
will be able to extinguish all the flaming arrows of the evil
one.—**Eph. 6:16a**

Here Paul continued his metaphorical treatment of the Roman soldier's armor by discussing the fourth piece—his large rectangular shield. These shields had a convex surface measuring 2-1/2 feet wide by 4 feet long and were 2-1/2 to 4 inches thick. They usually were constructed of two wood planks glued together. The wooden frame was covered with canvas and overlaid with six layers of animal hides woven together. This rendered the shield strong, durable and nearly impenetrable. Metal edging was attached to the top and bottom edges to protect the shield when it rested on the ground.

The shield covered most of the soldier's body. The shield, like our faith, was never meant to be held next to one's side or behind the back. Therefore, faith, being a *defensive* piece of armor, should be out in front where it can cover the believer in every situation of life. Being positioned in front of the soldier, it is also in front of all the other pieces of armor.

Paul exhorted his readers to **take up** the shield of faith. This command indicates every believer can willingly pick up the shield of faith or lay it down.

Maybe you have become discouraged and have stopped believing in God to work in your life. It is not too late to pick up your shield and walk in faith again. Without your protective shield in front, there is nothing between you and the onslaughts of Satan and his demon hosts. Paul told Timothy: "...that by them you fight the good fight, **19** keeping faith and a good conscience, which some have rejected and suffered shipwreck in regard to their faith" (1 Tim. 1:18–19).

There is no way we can successfully live the Christian life without giving attention to the development of our faith.

Thought for the Day: Are you giving daily attention to the health and development of your faith?

Notes:

_____

_____

_____

_____

_____

_____

TAKE UP THE SHIELD OF FAITH—PART II

*In addition to all, taking up the shield of faith with which you will be able to extinguish all the flaming arrows of the evil one—***Eph. 6:16b**

Yesterday we looked at Paul's admonition to take up the shield of faith. Today we will consider the many dangers of Satan's flaming arrows.

Maintenance of the shield was a daily duty of each soldier. Every day the soldier would rub oil into its outer covering of leather to keep it soft, supple and pliable.

Paul noted that the Evil One (Satan) shoots **flaming arrows** at the believer. Flaming arrows can represent literal arrows shot, as well as spears or javelins hurled at the soldier.

Arrows probably refer to spears whose shafts were approximately five feet long having iron tips about two feet long. Sometimes these spear tips were wrapped with tar, smeared with pitch, and ignited. Consequently, they became "flaming" spears with a killing range of approximately 100 feet. Upon impact, the tempered blade would sink into the shield and the soft spear shank would bend, making the shield difficult to handle. Sometimes the soldier would then abandon the shield, leaving himself unprotected.

"Flaming arrows" also may refer to three types of arrows commonly used in NT times. There were regular arrows, arrows dipped in tar and ignited, and hollow arrows filled with combustible fluids that burst into flames upon impact. *Flaming arrows* is a metaphor for every kind of attack launched by Satan and his hosts.

Some flaming arrows Satan can hurl at the believer include:

1. words, phrases, oaths

2. horrible language

3. temptations

4. vivid, evil imaginations that inflame and incite desires and passions

5. thoughts—of rebellion, doubt, malice, and fear.

Before the soldier went out to war, he placed his shield in a tub of water saturating the leather cover and canvas. By keeping your shield (heart and mind) saturated with the water of the Word, you will be ensured that every "flaming arrow" of the enemy will be quenched and deflected.

Thought for the Day: The only way to successfully deflect the flaming arrows of Satan is to take up your shield of faith!

Notes:

_____

_____

_____

_____

_____

_____

PUT ON THE HELMET OF SALVATION

And take the HELMET OF SALVATION.—Eph. 6:17a

Then Paul introduced the fifth piece of armor, the helmet of salvation. **Take** could also be translated *grab*, because the context seems to indicate the last thing a soldier did when he observed an approaching enemy was to grab his helmet and sword.

In Roman times, soldiers wore **helmets** of various shapes. They were made of bronze and were fitted over an iron skull cap that was lined with leather or cloth. The leather or cloth lining made the heavy helmet more bearable to wear. Some had cheek pieces, others had ornate engravings and etchings, and some were made to resemble the head of an animal. Others sported a plume of brightly colored feathers or horse hairs.

Paul likened **salvation** to the ornate, intricate helmet. No doubt Paul was drawing attention to the head, the mind, the brain, and the thinking processes of the Christian. The helmet protected the soldier's head. That is significant because Satan usually attacks Christians through their minds. Putting on the helmet of salvation involves daily increasing one's knowledge in two areas—the details of his/her salvation and the specifics of God's plan of salvation. These two steps may be accomplished by regular reading, studying and memorizing biblical passages.

Salvation can be viewed in three time frames—past, present and future. Each believer has been saved or justified by faith (past) and is being saved, which includes the present process of *progressive sanctification*. Third, the believer has not yet experienced complete salvation, sometimes referred to as glorification (in the future). Therefore, part of putting on the "helmet of salvation" is regularly reflecting on the *hope of salvation*. During spiritual warfare, Christians need to continually reflect on Jesus Who is their "hope of glory" (Col. 1:15)—or eternal life. This activity helps them persevere in the faith.

Thought for the Day: Do you usually wear the helmet of salvation?

TAKE THE SWORD OF THE SPIRIT

And the sword of the Spirit, which is the word of
God.—**Eph. 6:17b**

The sixth piece of armor Paul specified is the **sword of the Spirit**—the only *offensive* weapon. The soldier's sword possessed a razor sharp double-edged blade nineteen to twenty-four inches long and two inches wide. Consequently, it was well suited as a cut-and-thrust weapon for close combat. It was kept in a sheath attached to the loin belt on the right side of the body.

The sword could be used in battle in both defensive and offensive ways. Therefore, it could be used to repel or to attack the enemy. The other five pieces of armor provided protection for either the body as a whole or particular parts of it. The expression "sword of the Spirit" indicates the sword is empowered by the Holy Spirit as needed during spiritual warfare.

The Greek word for "word" indicates Paul has in mind the *spoken* or proclaimed **word of God**. This Greek word is used primarily to express confrontation and judgment. The spoken word of God is to be used against the spiritual wickedness of the devil. Jesus demonstrated this verbal or spoken use of the written word against the devil during His temptation in the wilderness (Matt. 4:1–11). God's inspired word has *cutting power*, being sharper than any two-edged sword (Heb. 4:12).

The Holy Spirit is a key theme in verse 17. First, the Holy Spirit helps us understand and interpret His Word (John 16:13). Second, the Spirit enables believers to use the Word of God (sword) properly during spiritual warfare.

Paul's exhortation is directed to both the individual believer and to the church, the corporate body of all believers.

Thought for the Day: Is your spiritual sword sharp and ready for use?

PRAYING AT ALL TIMES IN THE SPIRIT

With all prayer and petition pray at all times in the Spirit, and
with this in view, be on the alert with all perseverance and
petition for all the saints. —**Eph. 6:18**

Here Paul described "prayer" as a foundational and *continuous* activity that is critical to putting on all the pieces of spiritual armor. Consequently, prayer is at the heart of spiritual warfare. **With all prayer and petition** indicates Paul was thinking of every form of prayer. Some common categories of prayer include: adoration, thanksgiving, confession, and intercession.

The phrase **praying at all times** involves a present participle. Believers need to be in a constant state of prayer, because we do not know when we will come under a demonic assault. The phrase **in the Spirit** informed his readers how they were to pray. Their prayer is to be prompted and guided by the Spirit. Also, the Spirit prompts them to pray, shows them for whom to pray, instructs them *how* to pray, and energizes them in praying for themselves and others.

The clause **being on the alert with all perseverance and petition** implies an ongoing sense of expectancy that Christ's return could occur at any moment (Luke 21:36). Also, this phrase commanded believers not to become lazy about their prayer life. Perseverance and prayer are linked here and in other places (Rom. 12:12; Col. 4:2; Acts 1:14). Paul instructed his readers to intercede for **all** the saints. Paul used the word "all" four times in this verse: "pray at all times," "with all prayer and supplication," "with all perseverance," and "praying for all the saints." Paul's repeated use of all demonstrates the significance he attributed to *mutual, inclusive, and continual* prayer.

Thought for the Day: Believers need the intercessory prayers of fellow Christians if they are to "stand firm" (6:14) in the heat of spiritual battles. Are you praying for other believers?

ALSO, PRAY FOR ME!

*And pray on my behalf, that utterance may be given to me in the opening of my mouth, to make known with boldness the mystery of the gospel, **20** for which I am an ambassador in chains; that in proclaiming it I may speak boldly, as I ought to speak.—**Eph. 6:19–20***

Paul continued his emphasis on prayer by requesting his readers intercede for him. His two requests include: being given utterance (v. 19) and speaking boldly as he ought (vv. 19b, 20).

Paul's first request, **utterance may be given to me**, is in the passive voice which indicates words would graciously be given to him by God. Paul needed divine resources because of the spiritual warfare that came against his gospel ministry. Thus, Paul asked his readers to pray that utterance would be given him by God when he opened his mouth. *Utterance* refers to the correct word to speak when he opened his mouth to declare the gospel.

Paul's second request is that he will **make known with boldness the mystery of the gospel**. Paul desired the liberty of spirit to present the gospel clearly and boldly. The "mystery" involves the union of believing Jews and Gentiles into one body. Probably Paul made this request as he anticipated being brought out of jail and appearing before the supreme tribunal. Then he would have the opportunity of witnessing to Caesar with courage and clarity. Paul would have to defend the message of the "mystery of the gospel."

The fact Paul stated he was an **ambassador in chains** was *ironic*. Prisoners did not function in this role and ambassadors enjoyed a status of honor and prestige. Ambassadors have diplomatic immunity so they are able to **speak boldly** on behalf of the government they represent. Paul's two requests were appropriate for an ambassador, a representative of Jesus Christ.

Thought for the Day: Are you an effective ambassador for Christ?

PAUL'S CONCLUDING COMMENTS

But that you also may know about my circumstances, how I am doing, Tychicus, the beloved brother and faithful minister in the Lord, will make everything known to you. **22** I have sent him to you for this very purpose, so that you may know about us, and that he may comfort your hearts. **23** Peace be to the brethren, and love with faith, from God the Father and the Lord Jesus Christ. **24** Grace be with all those who love our Lord Jesus Christ with incorruptible love—**Eph. 6:21–24**

Paul usually closed his epistles with a series of personal remarks and greetings. However, Ephesians contains only one sentence of personal remarks (vv. 21–22) and *no* greetings. Paul's prayer, that can be considered a benediction, contains two invocations:

- for peace and love   v. 23

- for grace and immortality   v. 24

Paul gave two reasons for sending Tychicus to them. First, to give them a firsthand report of what is happening to Paul and other believers in Rome; second, to encourage their hearts. Tychicus was closely associated with Paul during the latter part of his ministry. In this context, **brother** means co-worker. Sending Tychicus to them showed Paul's pastoral concern.

Peace be to the brethren, and love with faith

Peace holds a prominent position in his benediction. Paul prayed that his readers would experience an ongoing, deeper level of peace from God the Father and Jesus. Peace is closely associated with reconciliation (2:14–18).

In addition to peace, Paul prayed for God's **love** to be poured out in a deeper measure on his readers. The third blessing Paul prayed for was their **faith**. Faith would be mandatory in their struggle to stand against powerful supernatural forces (6:16). Paul reminded them the source of peace, love, and faith is God—and the Lord Jesus Christ.

In the second invocation (v. 24), Paul asked for the blessing of God's **grace** on all who are in a loving, intimate relationship with the Lord. He associated this grace with immortality. This indicated that they will receive God's grace in endless supply through all eternity.

Thought for the Day: Are you living with an awareness that you can have a foretaste today of eternal life through your close relationship with the Lord Jesus Christ?

Notes:

_____

_____

_____

_____

_____

_____

ABOUT THE AUTHOR

Don E. Atkinson was born and raised in Lincoln, NE. He attended Southern Nazarene University (formerly Bethany Nazarene College) and Colorado State University securing a Bachelor of Science degree. Later he completed his Master of Science degree at Texas A&M University. He completed a significant amount of coursework towards a Master of Divinity (MDiv) degree at Trinity Evangelical Divinity School (TEDS) and Midwestern Baptist Theological Seminary (MBTS).

He has been active in his local church teaching adult Bible studies and preaching, as needed. Married in December of 1982, Don has three grown children. Currently, Don and his wife reside near Lyons, NE.

We would like to hear from you. Please

send your comments or questions

about this book to us in care of

daybydayintheword.org

Or by mail to: Don E. Atkinson

Day by Day in the Word

1400 Highway 51

Lyons, NE 68308

Thank you.

Day by day

in the Word

114

Made in the USA
Lexington, KY
18 June 2019